BEND, OVERALL

a guide to Exploring the Area's Best!

By Scott Cook

Wall Street, circa 1910.

Copyright © 2004, Scott Cook
All rights reserved. No part of this book may be reproduced in any form without previous written permission from the author. Don't be cheap, buy a copy. The author worked hard to make sure it's worth your fifteen bucks.

ISBN: 978-0-9799232-1-0

All photography and words – Scott Cook

Cover design – Moria Reynolds
Back cover design and maps – Gary Asher, Maverick Publications, Bend
Interior layout and design – Jody Conners, Maverick Publications, Bend
Printing and binding – Maverick Publications, Bend

Want to buy a book, sell this book, or send a letter?

    Write: Bend, Overall
                18160 Cottonwood Rd. #610
                Sunriver, Oregon 97707
   e-mail: bendoverallguidebook@yahoo.com

COVER PHOTO: Tumalo Falls
Top inset: Golden-mantled ground squirrel
Middle: Forest spring
Bottom: Broken Top's lake

BACK COVER INSETS:
Top:
  Clear Lake, Petersen's, East Lake hotspring, shroom, Bachelor, Obsidian Falls
Bottom:
  Lava Butte, kokanee, Tumalo SP, H.D. Museum, Green Lakes, Alder Sprgs

*DON'T PANIC – A tribute to the late Douglas Adams for writing the funniest hitchhiker's guidebook the galaxy has ever seen!

Warning: Hiking in Central Oregon is dangerous. All the information in this guide has been personally checked by the author to be accurate as of summer 2003. Trail conditions do change though – trees fall, land slides, volcanoes erupt, signs disappear, fees change. The author can accept no responsibility for any inconvenience, injury, or pregnancy due to the use of this guide.

BEND, OVERALL

WHADDAYA WANT FROM A GUIDEBOOK?

A fountain of moss? (22)
A rhyolitic erection? (51)
Battling hook-jawed fish? (52)
Two heads better than one?(40,42)
An underwater forest? (37)
Beaver-chewed juniper? (46, 50)

A floating iceberg? (19, 27)
A mini Grand Canyon? (44)
A two-headed fish? (41)
An octopus in a cave? (38)
A solar flare? (9)
New Zealand? (36)

A rock spirograph? (2)
A lava castle? (31, 45)
A bald eagle? (9, 14, 41)
A cavebeam? (28)
A monkeys face? (46)
A rubber biscuit (bowbowbow)

Bend, Overall is sort of a greatest hits packaging of Mother Nature's finest, generally within an hour's drive of Bend. Read every story – this is more than JUST a hiking guide! While it does include museums, resorts, and tourist attractions, it leaves out commercial endeavors unless they are one-of-a-kind. More than anything, this guide attempts to honor and showcase the variety and diversity of attractions and landscapes surrounding Bend.

Often guidebooks are long and narrowly focused in their attempt to be the "definitive" guide to an area. Not *Bend, Overall*. It does not include every hike and attraction in this area – just a sample of some of the best. It strives to be discriminating and succinct also, and thus, the arbitrary one-hour drivetime cut-off. Of course there are tons of excellent places just a bit further – been to the Painted Hills, White River Falls, Iron Mtn, Cougar Hot Springs, Derrick Cave, Warm Springs Museum, Glass Buttes, or Waldo Lake? You get the point – this area is blessed with a lifetime's worth of ventures, but a guidebook listing everything becomes cumbersome and expensive.

This guide is meant to be used in conjunction with a sense of humor and playfulness. There is no rule that says guidebooks should be dry and humorless. Laugh at my captions, grimace at my peculiarities, smirk at the naked people!

This short and pocket-sized **sampling** of the area's best is hopefully written with enough enthusiasm to inspire some new explorations. Go somewhere you've never been. I want to inspire people to celebrate our wonderful landscapes with unbridled joy. Write me a letter telling me what you think of *Bend, Overall.* Send me a photo of a secret place that you discovered – I want to know where everything is!

BEND, OVERALL

Table of Contents

- ❖ Using this Guide 6
- ❖ The MATRIX 7
- ❖ Trails Difficulty Scale 8
- ❖ Kids Love 9
  1. Pilot Butte 12
  2. Dry River Gorge 14
  3. Boyd/Skeleton Caves 16
  ?. Bare Lake 18
  4. High Desert Museum 20
  5. Deschutes River Trail 22
  6. Lava Butte 24
  7. Lava River Cave 26
  8. Lava Cast Forest 28
  9. Sunriver Nature Center 30
  10. LaPine State Park 32
  11. Paulina Creek Waterfalls 34
  12. Newberry Caldera Nat'l Mnmt 36
  13. Fort Rock/Hole-in-the-Ground 40
  14. Odell Lake Wildlife 42
  15. Tumalo Falls 44
  16. Mt. Bachelor 46
  17. Tumalo Mtn. 48
  18. Todd Lake 50
  19. Broken Top 52
  20. Sparks Lake 54
  21. Green Lakes Trail 56
  22. Devils Lake 58
  23. Sisters Mirror Lakes Loop 60
  24. Rock Mesa/Moraine Lake Trail 62
  25. Tam McArthur Rim 64
  26. Squaw Creek Falls 66
  27. North Sister - Thayer Glacier Lake 68
  28. Skylight Cave 70
  29. Black Crater Trail 72
  30. Matthieu Lakes Trail 74
  31. Dee Wright Observatory 76
  32. Obsidian Trail 78
  33. Tenas Lakes/Scott Mtn. Trail 80
  34. Linton Lake/Falls 82
  35. Proxy Falls 84
  36. Sahalie/Koosah Falls 86
  37. Clear Lake 88
  38. Sawyers Caves 90
  39. Canyon Creek Meadows/Jack Tr 92
  40. Head of the Jack 94
  41. Wizard Falls Hatchery/Metolius R Tr 96
  42. Head of the Metolius 98
  43. Black Butte Trail 100
  44. Alder Springs Trail 102
  45. Petersen Rock Gardens 104
  46. Smith Rock State Park 106
  47. Steelhead Falls 108
  48. Lake Billy Chinook 110
  49. Richardson's Rec Ranch 112
  50. Rimrock Springs Trail 114
  51. Stein's Pillar Trail 116
  52. Kokanee Spawn 118
- ❖ Drive Tour 1 - Cascade Lakes Hwy 120
- ❖ Drive Tour 2 - McKenzie/Santiam Passes 122
- ❖ Drive Tour 3 - Rocks and Irrigation 124
- ❖ Drive Tour 4 - Downtown Bend 126
- ❖ Art Hunt 128
- ❖ Tree Identification 130
- ❖ Topo Map 1 - Cascade Lakes Hwy 134
- ❖ Topo Map 2 - McKenzie Pass 136
- ❖ Topo Map 3 - Deschutes River/Lava Butte 138
- ❖ Topo Map 4 - Canyon Creek Mdws/Newberry 139
- ❖ Topo Map 5 - Squaw Creek/Tam 140
- ❖ The MATRIX Revisited 143
- ❖ Bend Map 142

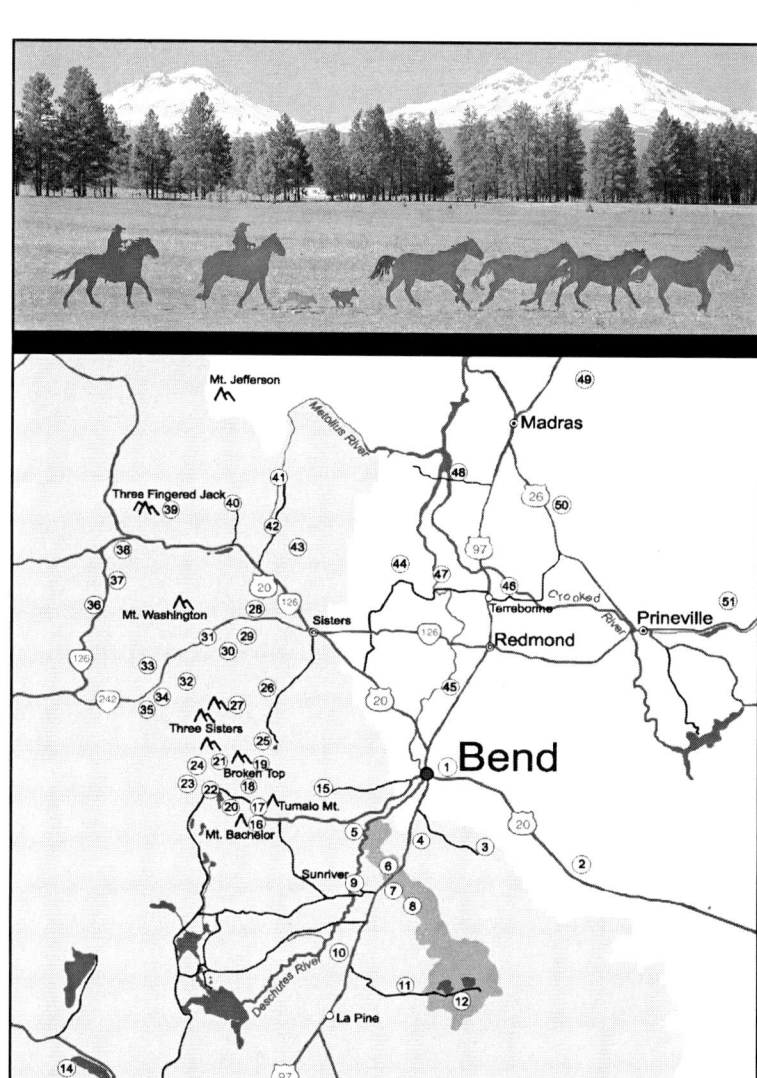

Anticipated praise for ***Bend, Overall***:

...a genre-busting literary masterpiece...

...an instant Oprah's list, page turning, edge-of-the-seat, thrill-a-minute, spellbinding roller-coaster ride...

...a staggering work of heartbreaking genius...a dazzling synthesis of contemporary thought...

*If you only read one book this year, it better be **Bend, Overall**!*

– Scott Cook, poor author

BEND, OVERALL

- Drive Time from Bend: x min
- Total Outing Time Guess: x hrs
- Trails: x
- Fee: x
- Dogs: x
- Bathroom: x

Map p. x

Using this Guide

Drive Time from Bend: This is the exact time it takes to drive to the entry from some imaginary spot in Bend.

Total Outing Time Guess: This includes the drive there and back and a real-life guesstimate of how much time an idealized person might spend there. Consult the Matrix, it knows everything.

Trails: A brief description of the difficulty and length of the trail(s).

Fee: $5 NW Pass – buy at outdoor retailers or at popular trailheads. Annual pass is only $30.

$3 S.P. – State Park fee payable at park entrances.

Dogs: Yes: no restrictions on dogs.

No: no dogs allowed – don't bring dogs into the caves.

Leash: There are two areas near Bend that have summertime leash laws. The Deschutes River Trail (entry 5) from 5 / 1 thru 10/1. The Three Sisters Wilderness entries 18, 19, 21, 23, 24 have a strictly enforced leash law from 7/1 thru 10/1.

DOGS REQUIRED TO BE ON LEASH

Maps: Topo maps featuring roughly half the entries begin on page 134. Included maps are an attempt to give perspective rather than having a small map for each entry. Maps are from the FS Ranger District maps – huge, inexpensive, awesome maps available at FS offices or at Bend Map and Blueprint (downtown, on Bond).

Driving Directions: From Bend, mileages start at either (going south) Third St. and Parkway. (Casc Lks Hwy) the roundabout at Century and Mt. Washington. (Going north) Hwy 97/20 junction. (McKenzie/Santiam passes) west end of Sisters at Hwy 242/20 junction.

Useful Phone Numbers:

Bend/ Fort Rock Ranger Dist:
541-383-4000

BLM Prineville Office:
541-416-6700

Sisters Ranger Dist:
541-549-2111

Crooked Riv Natl Grsslnd:
541-475-9272

McKenzie Ranger Dist:
541-822-3381

Oregon State Parks:
503-378-6305

Using The MATRIX

The Matrix indexes both the time an entry takes, round-trip from Bend, and the features of the entry. The time estimates range from a half-hour down to six hours. Built into the time estimates are some leisure time – the estimates are not the bare minimum time required.

But here are two generalizations; 1) The top half of the Matrix is skewed towards a quicker, time-constrained visit. Meaning that if you've got a tight schedule, you're probably not out to mosey, photo, and snack – thus the Deschutes River Trail is only 1.5 hours and the Todd Lake estimate of 1.5+ hours only gives you about 45 minutes at the lake, just enough for a brief look-see.

2) The bottom half of the Matrix's time estimates are skewed towards a more leisurely appreciation of the excursion. For example, Lake Billy Chinook is 5 hours – a brief visit could only take 2.5 hours, but the estimate assumes that people going that far will want to hike, boat, or sight-see and picnic. Also, Black Butte's estimate at 4 hours gives you about an hour at the summit to take in all the sights while eating and relaxing.

The Matrix is also a quick reference for a specific feature. Scan down a column for a rundown of waterfalls or fees or dog-friendliness.

The Matrix is perfect, always. No doubting allowed. *Hail the Matrix!*

Time Estimate MATRIX

Round-Trip Time Estimate from Bend (includes drive)

Time	Destination	Scenic Hike	Mtn Views	Waterfalls	Lakes	Unique Attraction	Drive Time (one-way)	Dogs	Fee
.5 Hr ↓	Mirror Pond				●	●	3	Y	
	McKay Park					●	4	Y	
	Pilot Butte - drive (1)		●				6	L	
	Town Tour								
1.0 Hr — ↓	Tumalo Falls View (15)			●			15	L	●
	Pilot Butte Hike (1)	●	●				6	L	
	Deschutes River Sites (5)	●		●			10	L	●
	Boyd Cave - sample (3)					●	12	N	
	Lava Butte (6)	●	●			●	9	L	●
	Petersen Rock Gardens (45)					●	11	L	
	LaPine S.P.-Big Tree view (10)					●	26	Y	
1.5 Hrs ↓	Boyd or Skeleton Cave (3)					●	12	N	
	Head of the Metolius (42)		●			●	35	L	
	Todd Lake (18)	●	●		●		25	L	●
	Sparks Lake (20)	●	●		●		27	Y	●
	Lava Cast Forest (8)	●	●			●	30	L	●
2 Hrs — ↓	Sunriver Nature Center (9)					●	18	L	●
	Lava River Cave (7)					●	10	N	●
	Dee Wright Observatory (31)	●	●			●	40	L	
	Wizard Falls Hatchery (41)					●	45	L	
	Skylight Cave (28)					●	40	N	
	Sawyers Cave (38)					●	51	N	
	Head of the Jack (40)	●					40	Y	
	Dry River Gorge (2)	●					20	Y	
2.5 Hrs ↓	Rimrock Springs (50)	●	●				46	L	
	Devils Lake (22)	●			●		30	Y	●
	Tumalo Mtn (17)	●	●				23	Y	
	Mt. Bachelor - Chairlift (16)		●			●	24	N	●
3 Hrs — ↓	Sahalie/Koosah Falls (36)	●		●			60	Y	
	Proxy Falls (35)	●		●			60	Y	
	Smith Rock S.P. (46)	●	●				28	L	●
	Steelhead Falls (47)	●	●				43	Y	
	High Desert Museum (4)					●	5	N	●
	LaPine S.P. Hike/Bike (10)	●	●				26	Y	
	Tumalo Falls - Hike (15)	●		●			15	Y	●
	Metolius River Canyon (41)	●					45	Y	
3.5 Hrs ↓	Mt. Bachelor - Summit Hike (16)	●	●				23	Y	
	Alder Springs (44)	●					41	Y	
	Squaw Creek Falls (26)	●		●			60	Y	
	Sisters Mirror Lakes (23)	●	●		●		30	Y	●
	Rock Mesa/Moraine Lake (24)	●	●		●		30	L	●
	Matthieu Lakes (30)	●	●		●		40	Y	●
	Richardsons Rec. Ranch (49)					●	60	Y/N	
	Clear Lake (37)	●	●		●		57	Y	
	Steins Pillar (51)	●					60	Y	
	Paulina Creek Falls (11)	●		●			28	Y	
	Fort Rock/Hole ITG (13)	●	●				70	Y	
	Tam McArthur Rim (25)	●	●		●		50	Y	●
4.0 Hrs —	Black Butte (43)	●	●				44	Y	●
	Linton Lake & Falls (34)	●		●	●		59	Y	●
	Newberry Caldera (12)	●	●		●	●	36	Y	●
	Broken Top (19)	●	●		●		45	L	●
↓	Green Lakes (21)	●	●		●		28	Y	●
5 Hrs ↓	Black Crater (29)	●	●				36	Y	
	Canyon Creek Meadows (39)	●	●		●		60	Y	●
	Lake Billy Chinook (48)	●	●		●	●	42	L	●
6 Hrs	Tenas Lakes/Scott Mtn (33)	●	●		●		50	Y	●
	Obsidian Trail (32)	●	●				51	Y	●
	North Sister - Thayer Lake (27)	●	●				43	Y	●
	Odell Lake Wildlife (14)				●	●	90	Y	

Hiking Difficulty Scale

BEND, OVERALL

Totally subjective! Difficult for one person is easy for another. Every guidebook has different criteria for when a trail moves from "easy" to "moderate" or from "mod" to "difficult". Some guides then use topography graphs and cumulative elevation gains to try to objectify their ratings, but these usually only appeal to people who hike all the time and consequently are fit enough not to need the charts anyway. Which is easier, a slight grade at 7,000 feet or a short steep at 3,623 feet? Is 10 miles of up and down more moderate than a loose scramble up a moraine slope? Who is John Galt?

This scale lists every hike in this guide in order of their difficulty. It is an attempt to lend perspective—one hike's difficulty compared to another's. Do a hike then check its position in this scale to see if its rating is in line with your experience, then decide if you want easier or harder next time.

Note: any hikes within a few positions of each other in this chart can be assumed to be interchangeable. This chart is an attempt to give a general sense of how a hike's difficulty rates, rather than an exact relation to another hike.

EASY
- Benham Falls (5)
- Metolius River - Head (42)
- Lava Cast Forest (8)
- Lava Butte (6)
- Head of the Jack (40)
- Smith Rock - river or bluff (46)
- Sparks Lake - Atkeson (20)
- LaPine State Park (10)
- Proxy Falls (35)
- Sahalie/Koosah Falls (36)
- Rimrock Springs (50)
- Todd Lakeshore (18)
- Metolius River Canyon (41)
- Fort Rock/Hole (13)
- Clear Lake (37)
- Paulina Lakeshore (12)

MODERATE
- Alder Springs - Short (44)
- Pilot Butte (1)
- Big Obsidian Flow (12)
- Squaw Creek Falls (26)
- Dry River Gorge (2)
- Deschutes River Trail (5)
- Linton Lake (34)
- Paulina Creek (11)
- Bare Lake (??)
- Steelhead Falls (47)
- Todd Lake Ridge (18)
- Canyon Creek Meadows (39)
- Tenas Lakes/Scott Mtn (33)
- Alder Springs - Long (44)
- Sisters Mirror/LeConte (23)
- Matthieu Lakes (30)
- Tumalo Falls - Happy Valley (15)
- Stein's Pillar (51)
- Mt. Bachelor - Lodge (16)
- Billy Chinook - Tam-a-Lau (48)
- Rock Mesa/Moraine Lake (24)
- Broken Top (19)
- Smith Rock - Misery Ridge (46)
- Green Lakes (21)

DIFFICULT
- Tumalo Mtn (17)
- Tam McArthur Rim (25)
- Obsidian Trail (32)
- North Sister - Thayer (27)
- Linton Lake - Upper Falls (34)
- Smith Rock - Burma Loop (46)
- Black Butte (43)
- Paulina Peak (12)
- Black Crater (29)
- Mt. Bachelor - Summit (16)

BEND, OVERALL
KIDS LOVE....

Town Tour (page 126) McKay Park for tubing and wading in the Deschutes.
Juniper Park for the playground, swimming pool, sports, and spacious grassy areas.
Mirror Pond for its space and chance to feed and harrass the geese.

3) Boyd and Skeleton Caves: fun if everyone is dressed warmly and has their own flashlight.

4) High Desert Museum: kids go crazy for all the wildlife, the puppet room, and the chance to ask questions and participate at the presentations.

6) Lava Butte: interesting short hikes. Check out the fire lookout and feed the squirrels at the summit picnic tables.

7) Lava River Cave: Lanterns for rent. The cave is pretty long – warm clothes and their own flashlights keep kids excited.

8) Lava Cast Forest: they like to climb and crawl in the tree casts, and the one-mile length and map keep things moving.

9) Sunriver Nature Center: lots of hands-on kids displays, plus the popular telescopes and bald eagle.

11) Paulina Creek Falls: First waterfalls are about 1.5m up from McKay, or just play and picnic at McKay campground and its waterfall.

16) Mt. Bachelor Chairlift: kids love it! The ride and restaurant make for a great family outing.

18) Todd Lake: a bit chilly for adults, but shallow for all-ages wading. Independent kids may be able to hike the lakeshore trail by themselves.

20) Sparks Lake: Shallow and warm for all kinds of splashing, wading or rafting. Maybe a first canoe or kayak trip.

31) Dee Wright Observatory: they love the weirdness of the castle and its view windows for a short stop.

35) Proxy Falls: Short enough with a variety of trees, lava, and waterfalls to keep kids excited.

36) Sahalie/Koosah Falls: a short path between two big falls.

37) Clear Lake: kids love paddling rowboats and eating in the homey café.

40) Head of the Jack: run and play and splash across the creek on the logs…the creek's not deep enough to worry about if they fall in.

41) Wizard Falls Hatchery: fish-feeding frenzy for a buck, plus some bonus curiosities and lunkers.

45) Petersen Rock Gardens: picnic and play hide 'n' seek while pestering the roosters and peacocks.

47) Steelhead Falls: mostly for teens who can jump and swim competently.

49) Richardson's Rock Ranch: Every kid loves thundereggs. Happiness is digging their own and having it cut – only for a couple of bucks.

STROLLER FRIENDLY PLACES

1) Pilot Butte	10) LaPine State Park	42) Head of the Metolius
4) High Desert Museum	20) Sparks Lake trail	45) Petersen Rock Gardens
5) Deschutes River Trail	31) Dee Wright Obs.	46) Smith Rock
6) Lava Butte	37) Clear Lake	50) Rimrock Springs
8) Lava Cast Forest		

BEND, OVERALL

DEDICATION

This guidebook is dedicated to the passion, courage and actions of the late Tom McCall, Governor of Oregon 1967-1975. Few men have the will, vision, or the means to shape the world to their view. We, here in Oregon today, are fortunate that Tom McCall had the will to shape Oregon. If you love Oregon, read his biography *Fire at Eden's Gate*, by Brent Walth. Tom McCall is a man worthy of tribute and remembrance.

THANK YOUS

I needed a lot of help to get this guide in print! So many friends endured being guinea pigs for my verbiage – I'd endlessly ask, "mossy idyll or sylvan retreat? Far-ranging vistas or sightlines sweeping the horizon? Precipitous bluff or towering cliff?" Thanks to all who threw their two cents in!

Thanks to Clif Bar and Jenny Naftulin for supplying a summer's worth of energy. Simply knowing that I had another Black Cherry Almond or Lemon Poppyseed in my pack often kept me going those extra miles to make sure my directions were exact. Without Clif Bars I might have panicked!

Thanks to Camelbak for supplying me a HAWG hydration pack. I asked for a pack that would hold two cameras, tripod, food, water, notebooks, etc. They sent a HAWG and it ruled! It's very comfortable and the design is intelligent – the water pouch is separated from the other pouches so that my cameras and notes were protected from accidentally abrading the water pouch. And it keeps a six-pack cold for the hike to one of our lounge-able lakes – I totally recommend it.

Thanks to Gary Asher and Jody Conners at Maverick Publications for holding my hand and making my layout ideas a reality – I'd dream it up and they'd make it work. If you want to be a first-time author, go to Gary for help. He's good.

Thanks to Brad Whiting for lending me both a camera and a computer in my times of need. I appreciate the nudge he gave me into a more modern digital existence.

Thanks to Ariel Moody for a helpful and expert job reading over my entries and correcting many of my flaws, both grammatical and character. Being radically honest, I own up to all the fragments, run-ons, misplaced punc,tuation, etc that still remain. They are my fault – they are my "style" rather than her oversight.

Thanks to Moria Reynolds (of PO-CARD fame) for the cover design.

And, thanks to Rebecca, Niki, Mike, Yvonne, Felice, Tracey, Brad, Libby, Tanya, Tood, Dave, and Piama for hiking and exploring with me and being patient with my photography.

BEND, OVERALL

ABOUT THE AUTHOR

SWM, 41. Born and raised near Chicago. Degree in mathematics from Vanderbilt Univ. Currently splits his time between Bend, Hood River, and Mexico, though he considers all of Oregon his home. Passions include beauty, photography, kiteboarding, hiking, reading, thinking, travel, and women. ISO: a well-lived life.

...about my photos and sense of humor...

Some people may be shocked to see nakedness in a guidebook. Some people will think that I'm obsessed with nudity because of my references, my images and my innuendoes. I hope not, but...Oh well. I don't think that my images are sexy or sexual.

I do think that the nudity in certain photos reflects how some people prefer to enjoy the beauty and solitude of our Central Oregon landscapes. Being in the deep forest or at a wilderness lake SHOULD make you feel unfettered and free. I came across lots of people sunning and swimming in the buff while I "researched" this guide – happy, joyous folk. The bodies of men and women are two of Nature's most beautiful creations, and anyone, no matter their shape, who is enraptured enough by Oregon's beauty to shed their clothing in celebration, is OK by me. I figure that either happy and joyous people like to strip, or stripping makes people happy and joyous!

I hope that my photos and phrases encourage Bendites to go out into our wild lands and play like children do – naked and happily swimming, laughing, and sunning! Please be respectful of others. Don't be crude or a nuisance. Do find a place of peace and solitude. Feel the warm sun on your bare skin. Read an engrossing book. Share some wine and chocolate. Explore. Discover. Romance. Honor both Mother Nature and our human nature.

Roundabout at Century & Mt. Washington.

Scenic Hike/Scenic Drive/Bend's Landmark

1

- Drive Time from Bend: 3 min
- Total Outing Time Guess: .5 hr (drive)
  1.0 hr (hike)
- Trails: easy/mod 2m loop
- Fee: free
- Dogs: leash
- Bathroom: yes

Map p.126

Pilot Butte

Paris has a tower, Seattle's got a needle, Frisco sports a bridge, and Bend's got butte! Seems fitting that such an outdoorsy town would have a hike-able volcano as its landmark rather than some fabricated structure.

There are two simple ways to the top – either a mile long paved road or a mile long dirt trail. Each climbs to the top of the 480-foot butte and most people hike up one then down the other (beware of cars on the road). The view from the top is, of course, Bend Overall. The scenery comes with consequences though; 100-year-old Bend has gone from range town to lumber mill town to recreation/tourism/retirement town. From atop Pilot Butte everybody ponders the pros and cons of present-day, population-boom Bend. So, instead of spewing some guidebook-speak about "magnificent panorama" or "ubiquitous Hi-Desert flora", here's some population and Bend/USA history to mull over on our town hike.

DRIVE The park is located on Greenwood Ave./Hwy 20 east of Third St. The road up the butte is on the western side whereas the parking area is accessed via the first left turn east of the butte (follow the signs).

- **Bend Elevation:** 3,623 feet
- **Incorporation Date:** Jan. 1905
- **Rainfall:** Bend –12 inches/year,
  Cascade crest – 100 inches/year

Deschutes County 2000-2025 Coordinated Population Forecast					
Year	Bend	Redmond	Sisters	Unincorporated County	Total County
2000	52,800	15,505	975	47,320	116,600
2005	69,004	21,838	1,777	53,032	145,651
2010	81,155	28,171	2,405	59,127	170,858
2015	91,462	34,503	3,003	65,924	194,892
2020	102,625	40,836	3,776	73,502	220,739
2025	111,925	47,169	4,688	81,951	245,733

YEAR	POP.	HISTORY	
1904	300	1903:	Wright Bros. fly at Kitty Hawk
		1904:	Crater Lake becomes Nat'l Park
		1908:	Ford Model-T rolls nationwide
		1909:	Power Dam built, electrifying Bend, creating MirrorPond
1910	536	1911:	Railroad arrives in Bend
		1916:	Brooks-Scanlon, Shevlin-Hixon Lumber Mills open. First population boom!
		1914-19:	World War One (USA enters 1917)
1920	5,415	1919-33:	Prohibition
		1922:	Road built up Pilot Butte promoting tourism
1930	8,848	1929-33:	Great Depression
		1938:	Santiam Pass opens – *Bulletin* declares "Bend moves closer to ocean"
1940	10,021	1939-45:	World War Two (USA enters 12/7/41 – Pearl Harbor)
1950	11,409	1950:	Brooks-Scanlon buys out Shevlin-Hixon, closes S-H mill
		1958:	Mount Bachelor Ski Area opens
1960	11,936	1962:	Hwy 97 moved from Wall St. to Third St.
		1964-65:	Astronauts train in lavalands near Bend
		1965-73:	Vietnam War
		1967-75:	Governor Tom McCall shapes modern Oregon
		1969:	Woodstock. Neil Armstrong, first man on moon
1970	13,710	1977:	Elvis dies
		1978:	Sun Country runs first commercial raft trip on Deschutes
1980	17,200	1981-85:	Bhagwan Shree Rajneesh turns Antelope into Rajneeshpuram and poisons The Dalles
1990	20,469	1990:	Newberry Caldera becomes Nat'l. Monument
		1994:	Brooks-Scanlon (Crown-Pacific) mill closes permanently
		1997:	*The Source Weekly* debuts
2000	52,800	1999:	Bend's first roundabout is built at Century Dr. & Colorado Ave.
2001	55,080	2001:	Bend Parkway opens 8/22/01
2002	57,750		
2003	62,900		*Bend, Overall* released 7/15/04

WHATEVER WHATEVER WHATEVER WHATEVER WHATEVER WHATEVER WHATEVER WHATEVER WHATEVER WHATEVER

Rumor has it that on summer full-moon nights an ever-increasing bunch of lunatics hike up the Butte near midnight – Naked! Everyone's welcome, flashlights unnecessary and discouraged. Shy folk wear hats.

Scenic Hike/Basalt Canyon

2
- Drive Time from Bend: 20 min
- Total Outing Time Guess: 2.5 hrs
- Trails: easy/2m 1-way hike
- Fee: free
- Dogs: yes
- Bathroom: no
- Seasonal closure

Dry River Gorge

Quite a curious gorge! Dry River Gorge is the extinct waterway that emptied the Ice Age "Lake Millican". This lake filled the basin SE of Horse Ridge, surrounding Fort Rock (entry 13). Within the two million year Ice Age there were many cycles of warming which caused this pluvial lake to flood and overspill Horse Ridge, eroding a deep canyon on its way to the Crooked River.

Entering the Canyon.

Explore this gorge via a 2m trail meandering gently "upstream" on the canyon floor. This trail weaves among boulders and ancient junipers until being blocked by tumbled-down basalt. Many small surprises await; colorful spring wildflowers, striped banding on the steep walls, and, at the turnback point, a couple of very out-of-place ponderosas. Sharp eyes may even spy a raptor or feral sheep.

Strangest of all is an array of "modern" (1988) petroglyphs (never mentioned in most guides). Look for these about a five-minute walk upstream from the road-end campsites. Scan the basalt boulders on trail's left – the huge glyphs are easy to spot if you're looking. Hmmm... is this rock art or defacement? Will these be considered "art" 1000 years from now? Go take a look. Fall thru spring is best – summer's way hot.

Spirograph Pictoglyph.

DRIVE (Note: as you drive from Bend look for ponderosas. See any among the Badlands junipers?) From Third St. in Bend turn east on Greenwood/Hwy 20. Go 17m and just past MP 17 turn left onto the quarry road, then immediately right towards the gravel piles. Pass gravel piles towards canyon mouth and follow any of the braided rough dirt roads for about .75m until they merge and dead-end at some campsites.

Two Feral Sheep

NOTE The BLM closes this gorge each spring to protect nesting prairie falcons from human disturbance. Once the falcons have fledged their young the gorge is opened for exploring. Please respect the closure dates from March thru August. Call ahead to the BLM at 541-416-6700 for info or dates.

HIKE Trail begins as double-track at campsites. At the 2m mark there are two huge ponderosas marking the turnaround point (ponderosas generally need 14 inches of rain to grow – this canyon gets less than 10 inches… hmmm, odd).

"Curious Gorge" is a good guidebook to the Hood River area.

Spirograph, a toy for drawing geometric patterns, was introduced by Hasbro in 1965.

Undeveloped Caves

3
- Drive Time from Bend: 12 min
- Total Outing Time Guess: 1.5 hrs
- Skeleton closed: 10/15 - 5/1
- Fee: free
- Dogs: no
- Bathroom: no

Two explorable lava tubes only a couple of miles apart just SE of Bend. Overall, these are similar to Lava River Cave (entry 7) – both tubes contain easy walking, boulder scrambling, and metal staircases descending into each cave's opening. Unlike the L.R.C. though, these caves are unsupervised and uncrowded. Don't expect help if your lantern goes out or if your flashlight batteries die and you were too dumb to bring back-ups. There will be no help – you will die a slow and torturous death within the bowels of the earth and your corpse will desiccate into the next "skeleton". Hence, bring lots of lights and warm clothing!

Boyd Cave: Lots of variety for adventurers – sandy floor and jumbled floor, breakdown piles and crawlways. Boyd is close to 2000 feet long, but most people stop early at the first breakdown scramble or crawlway. Not you! This cave rewards curiosity – each hardship opens up more walkable terrain. The sandbank just in from the entrance is from contraction cracks in the ceiling, which let the sand in

Boyd's Crawlway

from above. Takes about 20 minutes to get to the end. Lanterns are tough to crawl with – flashlights/ headlamps are best in this cave. Note: this is the only cave in the area that is not closed in the winter for bat protection.

DRIVE From Bend take Hwy 97 south for just a quarter-mile past the Third St. stoplight. Turn left onto China Hat Rd. and go 9m. Just before the pavement ends at a cattleguard, turn left for Boyd on FS 242, then .2m to the cave. For Skeleton go .8m more, left onto FS 1819, then 1.5m of washboard to the cave.

Skeleton Cave: Named after the 1920's discovery of teeth and skulls from pre-historic mammals such as giant bears, wolves, horses, foxes, etc. The cave is about 3000 feet long and the first half has some of the easiest cave-walking around – try turning off your lights to see how far you can brave complete darkness. In places there's perfectly flat sand, but there are also two cave-ins to pick your way past. At the midpoint of the cave there is a lefthand side tunnel that crawlers can explore. The final half of

Inside Skeleton Cave.

the tube goes downhill and gets continuously rougher until becoming blocked by tumble-down. About 30 minutes one-way to the end.

Skeleton Cave's parking and entrance.

During prohibition bootleggers used Skeleton Cave to hide their stills and brew their booze. Nowadays Bend's booze is distilled on Wall St. at the Bendistillery. Perhaps someday marijuana will be grown downtown also!

Cold muddy lake

?
- Drive Time from Bend: ?
- Total Outing Time Guess: ?
- Fee: NW Pass
- Dogs: yes
- Bathroom: no

Bare Lake

Goldilocks caught these two bears. (Photo by Niki)

Bend's skinny-dippers love to go (to) Bare! The lake's playfully suggestive name is the real draw – as well as its off-the-path seclusion. Hardly scenic, Bare is a small shallow lake with some grassy shore and a muddy bottom. Not nearly as nice as the Sisters Mirrors, Tenas, Matthieus, or Moraine. But the clothes-free bunch embrace it to swim, float, and bask without bothering normal on-trail hikers. No tan lines, pickup lines, nor lines of tactiled tourists!

Thus, the catch…the "regulars" want more au-nature lovers to visit and play, but not at the expense of curious peepers disrupting their Bare. This lake is no better than hundreds of other Cascade lakes, so don't go to gawk – go to get nekkid and frolic on a raft. One bathing suit makes everyone overly self-conscious. C'mon Bend, grin and Bare it!

DRIVE These directions are meant to be purposely vague and sneaky. To find Bare requires extra effort – get there, get bare, and you'll be glad every Cascade Lakes Hwy tourist isn't there!

CLUES
1) Bare is on most topo maps, but not the ones in this guide.
2) It's about a half-mile hike from a popular (elev. 6150) lake.
3) This mountain's photo was taken barely a stones throw from the lake.

Now that you've figured it out, from the parking area go left around lake on the road/trail. In about seven minutes stop at a camp sign. Turn left, leave the trail and walk about 100 yards to a white gravel slope. Turn left and traipse up this steep hill thru the forest for about ten minutes. Good luck – bring a towel, floatie, drinx, lunch, and SPF. Beware; peeping people may be peppered with a peck of pinecones!

WHATEVER WHATEVER WHATEVER WHATEVER WHATEVER WHATEVER WHATEVER WHATEVER WHATEVER WHATEVER

There is no Oregon law which prohibits being nude on public lands. Extensive legal precedent nationwide concludes that mere nudity is not in itself lewd or indecent exposure.

Interpretive Zoo/Museum

4
- Drive Time from Bend: 5 min
- Total Outing Time Guess: 3 hrs
- Open: 9-5, 362 days
- Fee: $12 adults/$7 kids
- Dogs: no
- Bathroom: yes

Map p.138

High Desert Museum

Museum entrance.

A local treasure born out of a passion to preserve the natural and cultural landscapes of our High Desert. This nonprofit museum has thrived since 1982 on the enthusiasm it creates in kids and adults alike!

Typical of a museum, there are displays, photos, and artifacts. But unlike most museums this place is alive with all kinds of High Desert wildlife! Otter antics provoke laughter. Eagles, hawks, and owls inspire awe in the Birds of Prey wing—wow, at least 5 different types of owls. Porcupine feeding always draws a crowd to see the cute buggers munch. Snakes, bats, lizards, trout, and even mustangs round out this Great Basin zoo.

Outdoor porcupine habitat.

Because the intent of this museum is to "interpret" the High Desert environment, there are show-and-tell presentations given by passionate volunteers scheduled every day. These talks rule—plan your visit around them! Also, various exhibits detail the lives and history of the Plateau Indians and the encroaching settlers. A well-balanced perspective on the different cultures and how they clashed.

Baby porcupine chowing.

Overall, kids adore this place for its wildlife and adults marvel at the terrific job the museum does of informing without too much dull reading – quite a feat!

(DRIVE) From Bend take Hwy 97 south 4m. Past MP 145 turn left into signed entrance.

Everyone loves the cute screech owl.

(DETAILS)

- 3 hours are recommended.
- Little known fact – the admission price is good for two days. Stop in for a sample then return the next day with more time.
- The Rimrock Café offers good variety for great prices.
- Gift Shop is excellent – leave time for it.

Underwater otter antics.

WHATEVER WHATEVER WHATEVER WHATEVER WHATEVER WHATEVER WHATEVER WHATEVER WHATEVER WHATEVER

The Great Basin includes most of Nevada with bits of Oregon, Idaho, Calif., and Utah. Two deserts dominate the Basin – the northern high, or cold, desert and the southern low, hot desert. The High Desert, characterized by sagebrush, averages 4,000-6,000 feet of elevation. The low desert, dropping to minus 280 feet in Death Valley, features cactus and yucca.

Scenic Hike/Waterfalls/Drive-to Viewpoints

5

- Drive Time from Bend: 10 min
- Total Outing Time Guess: 1.5 hrs
- Trails: easy/9.6m (one-way)
- Fee: NW Pass
- Dogs: leash (5/1 - 10/1)
- Bathroom: yes

Map p.138

Deschutes River Trail

The nearest-to-downtown section of the mighty Deschutes with no pesky development lining its banks. Beginning at the Meadow Picnic area, a 9.6m hike or bike trail hugs the river while passing popular "waterfalls" Lava Island, Dillon, and Benham.

Besides the Meadow trailhead, there are spur roads off F.S. 41 leading to these popular spots:

Lava Island Falls: This is where most commercial raft trips take out. Lava from Lava Butte spilled into the river channel dividing the river around a lava island. Check-out the Indian rockshelter after reading the signboard. It's just a few hundred yards downriver. The rugged and curious may find a scramble trail down to a hidden falls just past the trio of info signs. Hike upriver .75 m to the Big Eddy class-3 rapids where rafts and kayaks spill.

Dillon Falls: A two-minute walk downstream brings you to a frothing chasm of certain death! Much more of a waterfall than Lava Island. Picnic tables, BBQs, bathrooms.

Benham Falls: The most scenic and geologically interesting place on the trail. A short path overlooks the Deschutes churning thru a narrow rhyolite defile. Here's an overview of the fascinating story told by this landscape: about 6000 years ago Lava Butte erupted (over by Hwy 97), forming a cinder cone and discharging a huge lava flow. The fluid lavas flowed west and blocked the bed of the ancient Deschutes with a 100-foot lava dam. A lake began backing up, extending south to LaPine, cov-

Benham Falls overlook.

ering the Sunriver area. Eventually the rising lake found a path around the lava and flowed over a low spot in much-older rhyolite rock. Since that time the re-routed river has been eroding its way downward in this channel, creating present-day Benham Falls.

Upriver from the falls you can take a stroll on a flat, easy half-mile railbed trail. Lava Butte is across river in the distance. Cross the bridge and check-out the logging history park – the whole deal takes about 45 minutes.

A kayaker at Big Eddy.

DRIVE From Bend take the Casc Lks Hwy for 4.7m. The Meadow Picnic area is signed before the Widgi Creek golf course. To access the falls, pass the Inn of the Seventh Mtn and turn left onto FS 41 at a sign for Deschutes River Rec. sites. Lava Island turnoff is .3m (then .7 gravel). Dillon is 2.5m (then .8 gravel). Benham is 3.8m (then 2.2 gravel). Benham is only 15 minutes from Bend, or it can be found from Lava Butte on Hwy 97.

Lava Island Falls rafting take-out

Many times this century an irrigation dam was proposed at Benham Falls. It would have backed-up the lake just like the lava dam did 6000 years ago. The ground was found to be too porous though. Sunriver is glad they built the dam at Wickiup instead.

Scenic Hikes/Mtn Views/Info Center

6
- Drive Time from Bend: 9 min
- Total Outing Time Guess: 1.5 hrs
- Trails: easy
- Fee: NW Pass
- Dogs: leash
- Bathroom: yes
- Open: 9-5 May thru mid-Oct

Map p.138

Lava Butte

This impressive red and black cinder cone "volcano" rises directly off Hwy 97 ten miles south of Bend. The butte is the home of the Lava Lands Visitor Center – the informational hub of the Newberry Volcanic Monument. Its staff of friendly people will answer all questions concerning Lava River Cave, Lava Cast Forest, and Newberry Caldera. Plus it contains a supply of maps, books, displays, and a video room. Two trails begin at the Center. The Trail of Molten Land provides an introduction and explanation of all things lava.

The must-see highlight is the butte itself. A 1.5m road spirals up to its 500-foot height. The rim has picnic tables, a crater filled with ponderosas, a .25m rim trail, and a fire lookout with a public room displaying panoramic mountain-identifying panels. Summertime can be crazy atop the butte – tons of kids happily feeding the swarm of hungry squirrels! For people looking for a bit more serenity, try hiking up to the butte (on the 1.5m road) after the Visitor Center closes at 5PM. Simply park inside the exit gate and walk through the lot then up the steady mile to the top. A Cascade sunset, fiery sky bathing the red cinders in warm light, only gets better by adding a boyfriend and a bottle of red wine! No mob like atop Pilot Butte, and the walk down in the dark is a breeze. A full-moonrise is deluxe!

Yvonne, Dave, Brad, Tood & Kona on a November outing.

DRIVE — From Bend take Hwy 97 south for 8m. At MP 149, south of the butte, turn right into signed entrance.

Fire lookout atop butte.

There are four common types of lava, each identified by its percentage of silica. Basalt has less than 54%, andesite has 54%-62%, dactite has 63%-72%, and rhyolite has more than 72%. The silica content determines the viscosity of the lava. Low silica basalt is very fluid and can flow far from its vent (Lava Butte or Belknap Crater). The other lavas are too thick to flow far, so they build up steeper "composite" cones (the major Cascade peaks).

Developed Cave

7
- Drive Time from Bend: 10 min
- Total Outing Time Guess: 2 hrs
- Open: 9am-5pm May thru Oct
- Fee: NW Pass
- Dogs: no
- Bathroom: yes

Map p.138

Lava River Cave

Ever spelunked for a mile? Bend's famous Lava River Cave is the place to begin your explorations of Central Ore.'s many lava tubes. Why? Because this cave is Oregon's longest walkable tube and its cave 'features' are unique and intriguing. There are signs/brochures/maps/rangers to answer questions, and lanterns for rent at the entrance.

This cave is not a sanitized walk-in-the-park though. The entrance is a long stairway descending over tumbled-down lava. Immediately you'll notice the 40-degree freeze – whoa, you better have solid shoes, pants, jacket, and maybe even hat and gloves if you plan to walk into the bowels of the earth! As eyes adjust the rough terrain gets easier to navigate but you realize that mucho light is mucho good. Everyone should carry some kind of light. It's way more fun lingering to suit your curiosity than it is to stumble after your friend's beam. Progressing into the depths, the brochure details the glories of this cave; Hwy 97 passing overhead, the rare tube-in-the-tube, the 'sand garden', and other lavacicle weirdities.

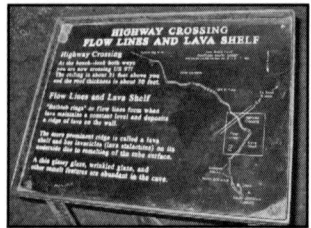

This cave is amazing – an easy, must-see family adventure!

Staircase and walkway inside entrance.

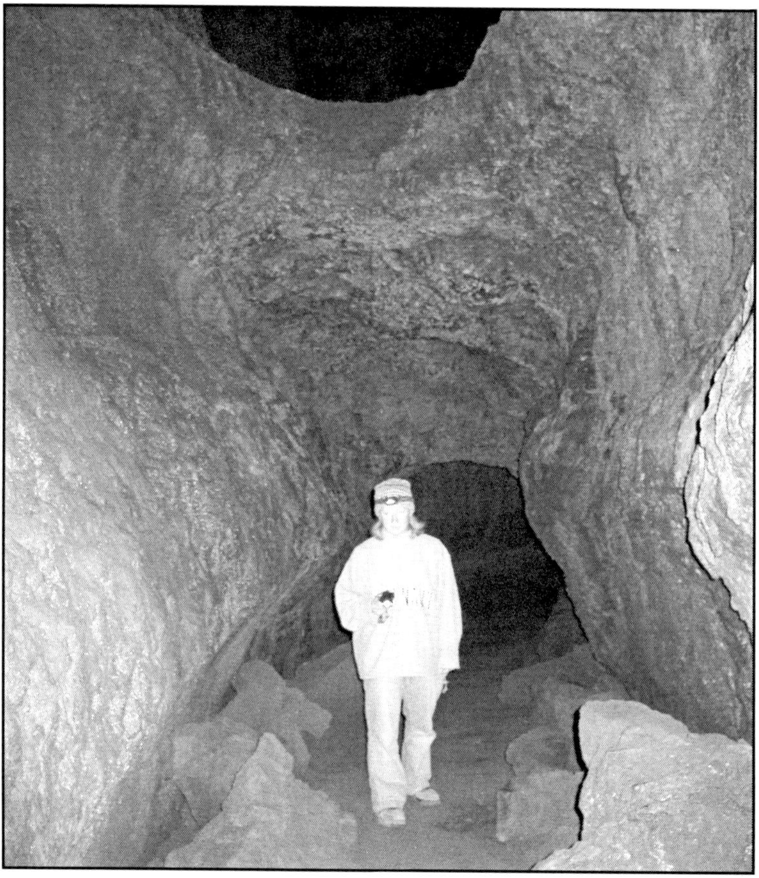

Tanya at the Tube within the Tube.

DETAILS

- To the end and back is a slow 2.2 miles – usually about 1.5 hours.
- No dogs, food, drinks, or smoking.
- Lantern rent is $3 (until 4PM). You can bring your own only if it doesn't have any glass.
- Use bathrooms outside – no bathroom inside cave. Don't pee in cave, it causes a gross white fungus to grow.
- Warm clothing is a must to be comfortable past 100 yards.
- Bring extra lights. People are always needing help because they stumble and break/put-out the lanterns. Bring a flashlight and also a lighter as backup.

DRIVE

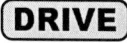

From Bend take Hwy 97 south 9m to MP 150. Signed entrance is on the left, just a bit past Lava Butte.

WHATEVER WHATEVER WHATEVER WHATEVER WHATEVER WHATEVER WHATEVER WHATEVER WHATEVER

"Spelunca" is Latin for cave.

WHATEVER WHATEVER WHATEVER WHATEVER WHATEVER WHATEVER WHATEVER WHATEVER EVER

Lava Cast Forest

Scenic Hike/Natural Wonder

8
- Drive Time from Bend: 30 min
- Total Outing Time Guess: 2 hrs
- Trails: easy/1m loop
- Fee: NW Pass
- Dogs: leash
- Bathroom: yes

Red-hot lava pours down the hillside and engulfs the forest. Fires dot a landscape embroiled in a hellish inferno! God flees as Satan dances on the corpse of Mother Nature – oops, scratch that, got carried away. Fires dot the landscape as molten lava surrounds and ignites the standing trees. The sluggish lava cools around the tree trunks before they fully burn…leaving…a Lava Cast Forest!

Pick up an interpretive map at the trailhead and tour these peculiar lava lands via an easy one-mile paved pathway. It snakes between numerous well-like "casts" and a collection of twisted trees. The likenesses of the long-gone trees are now cast in stone while their younger siblings live and die in a tortured tango atop the lava.

Exploring a kickass tree "cast".

As you stroll imagine Bend's cataclysmic landscape 7,000-8,000 years ago…Mt. Mazama (Crater Lake) blows its top and covers everything in feet of ash. Soon after, Newberry's 400 cinder cones sprout up and spew ash, cinder, and lava… the hillsides burn. Satan…oops. Lava Butte belches cinders and a huge lava flow which dams the Deschutes into a 20-mile lake. Whoa, bad times for local Indians.

Overall, this is a pretty neat hike for the whole family. Jungle-gym tree wells for the kids, good views and interpretation for adults. Two oddities of note: at sign #2 a misplaced fir amongst the pines and at sign #12 be sure to check out the fantastic re-melted molds.

(DRIVE) Note: In mid-summer the dirt road is very dusty washboard for the whole 9m.

From Bend speed south on Hwy 97 for 11m. At MP 153, across from the Sunriver entrance, turn left onto FS 9720. Follow signs on this gravel washboard for 9m to trailhead. (One mile in, on the right, you can explore a cinder pit.)

Well, well, well

WHATEVER WHATEVER WHATEVER WHATEVER WHATEVER WHATEVER WHATEVER WHATEVER WHATEVER WHATEVER

Washboard road is caused by your car's suspension. It dissipates the shock and energy of road irregularities with a bouncing rhythm called harmonic oscillation. At each downstroke the wheels exert extra force on the road, causing the particles in the road to either pack or displace at regular intervals. Once a pattern establishes it becomes self-reinforcing due to forced oscillation – the next car hits the bumps and bounces at the same frequency, further defining the pattern. Washboard is inevitable on dirt roads traveled by vehicles with suspension.

Museum-like attractions/Observatory telescopes

9
- Drive Time from Bend: 18 min
- Total Outing Time Guess: 2 hrs
- Hours: 9-5 daily
  Solar view 10am-2pm, Nightview 9-11pm ($6.00)
- Fee: $3.00/adults
- Phone: 541-593-4394
- Bathroom: yes

Sunriver Nature Center

Telescopes, bald eagles, meteorites, and critters. Sort of like a mini High Desert Museum, but not as extensive nor expensive. Some offbeat displays, a nature trail, and the fabulous Observatory make the Nature Center a fun educational stop for the whole family. Where else are you gonna see an eagle and a solar flare at the same place?

The Starport Observatory: Stare at the Sun – close-up! A research-grade telescope is fitted with special filters to enable this unforgettable experience. Available 10-2PM daily in the summer, included with admission price. The Observatory also has a little-known, yet excellent, nighttime star program. In summer it runs 9-11PM every night except Monday ($6/adult, $4/kid). Included is a fun slide presentation on astronomy while the numerous telescopes are focused on different nebulae, clusters, binaries, etc. If you ever wondered about the 5th Dimension's, "When the moon is in the 7th house, and Jupiter aligns with Mars…peace will guide the planets and love will steer the stars…This is the dawning of the Age of Aquarius," then the constellation Q and A is your ticket!

Warmly dressed nighttime crew.

The Nature Center: Displays contain local history, animals such as snakes, lizards, salamanders, and frogs, plus kids' hands-on exhibits. The meteorite nook is outta this world! Outside there's a self-guided nature trail with a view over to a bald eagle perched on its own island.

This place is worth a stop – everyone loves the sun and you'll probably find the rest more interesting than you'd think.

Great horned owl.

Spellbound!

DRIVE From Bend take Hwy 97 south for 12m. At MP 153 turn right towards Sunriver then 1.5m to the entrance. Now follow Nature Center signs through three traffic circles – turn at 3 o'clock in the first circle, 11 o'clock in the second, and 9 o'clock in the third.

WHATEVER WHATEVER WHATEVER WHATEVER WHATEVER WHATEVER WHATEVER WHATEVER WHATEVER WHATEVER

In Japan, they call the Pleiades star cluster "subaru", meaning "gathered together". If you watch the Pleiades set over the Three Sisters through your Subaru's sunroof, how many sisters would you have?

Scenic Hike/Monster Ponderosa

10
- Drive Time from Bend: 26 min
- Total Outing Time Guess: 1.5 hrs (tree)
  3.5 hrs (bike/hike)
- Trails: easy
- Fee: free
- Dogs: yes
- Bathroom: at tree

LaPine State Park

A mello place. Tranquility defines this large park bordering both the Deschutes and the spring-fed Fall River. Numerous trails meandering over very gentle terrain make for easy strolling or mtn-biking for the whole family.

Three popular reasons to visit this park are: 1) The Big Tree, 2) Fishing and camping on the Deschutes, 3) Trails to the crystalline waters of Fall River.

The Big Tree: Biggest ponderosa in the world! "Big Red", a massive yellowbelly punkin, lives a contented life just steps from the Deschutes. At close to 500 years old, this tree has seen everything ...except you. Go visit, he'll love your company.

Fall River Trail: At the McGregor Memorial sit and watch the Deschutes flow or begin a 4.75m loop trail

Big Red dwarfs the author.

Fall River's falls.

McGregor Viewpoint.

heading for Fall River and it's 10-foot falls. This hike offers flat terrain and solitude but no real views except the falls. Good for a family-speed mtn bike outing. A signboard details the route and signs along the way keep you on track.

Camping: Extensive RV-type sites. Plenty of prime riverside sites.

Fishing: Can't tell or the good spots wouldn't be good anymore.

DRIVE From Bend take Hwy 97 south for 20m. At MP 160 turn right at State Park signs. Big Tree is 4.5m then right onto gravel for .7m more. For McGregor, pass Tree and Day Use, cross river, then right at sign. Camping is further, past ranger station.

Ponderosa pines are the most widely scattered pine in North America – they grow in every western state. Scottish botanist David Douglas (of Douglas fir fame) named the tree for its "ponderous" size during his 1826 travels.

Scenic Hike/Waterfalls

11

- Drive Time from Bend: 28 min
- Total Outing Time Guess: 4 hrs
- Trails: mod/3m one-way
- Fee: free (from McKay)
- Dogs: yes
- Bathroom: yes

Map p.139

Paulina Creek Waterfalls

Some hot-day nectar! In Newberry Caldera East Lake percolates to Paulina Lake which then spills into Paulina Creek. The creek then tumbles 2200 feet in about 8 miles down to the Hwy 97 level. Happiness is… Paulina Lake spilling its warmish top waters to make the bounty of waterfalls along the creek warm enough for splashing and romancing fun!

The Peter Skene Ogden trail (named for Paulina Lake's 1826 discoverer) parallels the creek as it ascends 8.5m to Paulina Lodge. The trail can be hiked, biked, or horsed the whole length, but a 3-mile stretch in the middle gives the most bang for the hiking buck. This stretch, beginning at the McKay Camp waterfall, starts with an easy-going 1.5m through a 1988 burn. The next 1.5m the trail steepens, as does the creek. Steep creek means waterfalls, waterfalls mean smiles :-). You'll pass a variety of beauties (listen and bushwhack to find some really secret ones) until you reach a junction trail. It goes right, crossing a bridge to road 300. This marks the turnaround for this hike. After exploring the nearby gems, head back to bask in a favorite or continue about 4 more miles to Paulina Lodge (if you want a much longer outing).

Twin Falls.

DRIVE From Bend take Hwy 97 south for 20 m. At MP 161 turn left at signs for Newberry Caldera. Go 3m and turn left onto gravel at sign for McKay Campground. Go 2.2m, cross creek, and park at trailhead sign.

NOTE This hike should not be attempted by people who are no fun. Nor should it be attempted without cold beers stashed in the insulated pocket of your Camelback. This creek's for you!

McKay's 15-ft. falls.

Road 300 foot bridge.

WHATEVER WHATEVER WHATEVER WHATEVER WHATEVER WHATEVER WHATEVER WHATEVER WHATEVER WHATEVER

"Come visit us again and again. This is a state of excitement. But for heaven's sake, don't come here to live."

– Governor Tom McCall's famously incendiary 1971 quote, excerpted from his biography "Fire at Eden's Gate" (written by Brent Walth).

Scenic Hikes/Mtn Views/Waterfall/Lakes/ Lodges/Restaurants

12
- Drive Time from Bend: 36 min
- Total Outing Time Guess: 4 hrs
- Trails: easy/mod/diff
- Fee: NW Pass
- Dogs: yes
- Bathroom: yes
- Boat Rentals

Map p.139

Newberry Caldera Nat'l Mnmt

National Park debate raged for nearly a century; Crater Lake "won", Newberry "lost". This Caldera has the qualities of a National Park but "the powers that were" only granted it Monument grade. Their loss, our gain! Been to a National Park lately? High fees, crowds, rules, regulations, and RVs. No bikes, no dogs, no boats, no access blah blah blah. Crowd together on Old Faithful's bleachers, wait in line at Half Dome's ladder, frame the Grand Canyon between RVs and helicopters...whatever. Rejoice – here in our backyard we've got the joys without the hordes! Newberry Caldera is both an embarrassment of natural riches and a

Paulina Falls.

Yvonne peeks from the peak.

Lakeshore tubs with a view.

playground for people who like to "do". Bike or snowmobile, rent a boat, catch a big fish, drive or hike to a spectacular viewpoint, watch osprey fish while basking in a "secret" hot spring, marvel at Oregon's unique Obsidian flow, splash in Paulina Creek's many waterfalls. Camp, picnic, rent a cabin, or, outside the Caldera, climb a volcano, hop in a tree cast, or tour a cave – all for five bucks!

National Park neighbor, Crater, certainly offers unreal beauty and a quick refresher in German and Japanese, but it seems crowded and RV-touristy compared to Newberry's engaging opportunities. Few things make you happier to be in Central Oregon than a full day of Newberry's charms followed by an amazing Cascade sunset as you head home on Hwy 97. Tell all your friends…no wait, don't tell anyone.

Romance

Most visitors are locals bent on hooking a huge trout, but here are some highlights for the non-fish folks.

Note: when paying the NW pass fee at the entrance booth on the access road, you get a detailed map to guide and orient.

Paulina Peak: Without a doubt, Oregon's finest viewpoint. As your gaze sweeps 360-degrees words fail…but Carpenters lyrics spring to mind. "Sitting on top of the world", this 7,984-foot peak looks down on amazing creation – twin lakes and a frozen flow of black glass glimmer below. Clear morning air reveals Washington's Mt. Adams (168m distant,

Paulina Lodge.

just to the right of Mt. Hood). To the south peeks California's Mt. Shasta (165m), while to the SE Steen's Mtn. is a hump in the hazy distance – Wow! Most folks drive a 4m-gravel road to the peak, but hardy "doers" can venture up a 2m trail. It begins at the Crater Rim Trailhead, located .5m up road 500. Though it's a steep 1500-foot climb, the pleasure of solitude and the increasingly epic views make this a must for true hikers!

Big Obsidian Flow Trail: A .75m, 30-minute trail begins up 80 stairs then loops into the heart of this uniquely young obsidian wonderland. Surrounding you are crazy swirls and zigzagged bands of pumice and glass. Excellent interpretive signs enlighten and enliven – no boring lectures, just amazing facts and graphics! Tree sleuths should examine the dwarfed pines; 5-needle, 3-needle, and 2-needle also – neat! (Page 130). Don't miss this trail – it's a unique experience.

Signs on Big Obsidian.

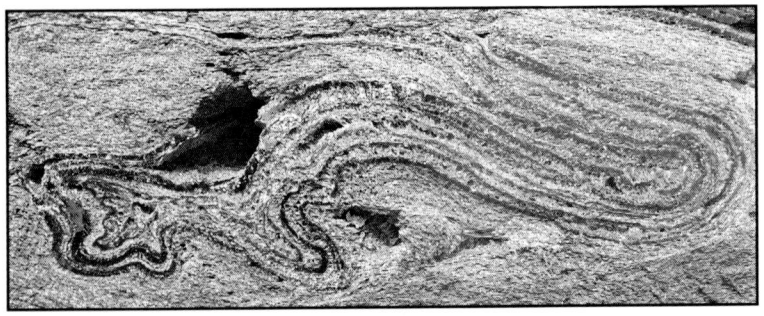
Obsidian swirl.

Paulina Lakeshore Trail: 7m of fairly easy trail circles the lake. The NE 3.5m between lodge and Little Crater camp is best for serenity, views, obsidian, and hot springs. The south section from the lodge travels past numerous summer houses and campgrounds – only worth it if you must loop. The best short O/B hike is the 1.5m going north from Little Crater to the red cinder hill – awesome scenery!

Paulina Lakeshore Trail.

Paulina Hot springs: Shoreline springs hotly seep up thru the pumice gravel "beach" just right of the red cinder hill (NE corner of lake). Enthusiasts dig out pools and line them with downed trees. Pools vary widely in temp., depth and use, but the outstanding sight of the Peak and Big Obsidian never fails. Fishing boats cruise the area so suit (or not) to taste – whichever feels right, there is no rule. Soak, swim, soak, smile! Find them about 1.25m from Little Crater or 2.25m from lodge. Unsigned spur trails lead down to the "beach" just as the trail begins going up the red cinder hill.

East Lake: Cabins, restaurant, store, boat rentals, boat ramp, nice people! Not only is the lodge's beach the best in the caldera, but the sand is mostly black obsidian – weirdly unique! Ask owners about "secret" hot springs on the shore of East Lake.

East Lake Resort.

Kokanee Spawn: See entry 52.

DRIVE From Bend take Hwy 97 south for 20m. At MP 161 turn left at signs for Newberry. Go 13m, passing and paying at booth, to Paulina Lake, lodge, and visitor info center. East Lake is just a few miles further.

WHATEVER WHATEVER WHATEVER WHATEVER WHATEVER WHATEVER WHATEVER WHATEVER WHATEVER WHATEVER

". . . the better people know this region, the better equipped they will be to decide the course of its future."

– Donald Kerr, High Desert Museum Founder

Scenic Hikes/Explorations

13

- Drive Time from Bend: 70 min
- Total Outing Time Guess: 4 hrs
- Trails: easy & mod rambling trails
- Fee: free
- Dogs: yes
- Bathroom: yes (at F.R. only)

Fort Rock/Hole-In-The-Ground

Two examples of a rare geologic phenomenon just miles from each other on the Lava Plains east of LaPine. Both are explosion craters caused by magma moving upwards in the earth's crust until contacting underground water. Without the presence of groundwater, a regular cinder cone would have formed instead. The Hole resulted from an underground explosion that spewed rock and ash into a perfect circle around the vent – called a tuff ring. It's a mile across, 425 feet deep, and was often mistaken for a meteor crater by pioneer scientists!

Sagebrush plains around Fort.

Fort Rock is similar, but it exploded beneath the waters of an Ice-Age lake that covered this basin until about 12,000 years age. The explosion built a tuff ring also, but the water and waves of the lake washed away all the ash. What's left is a circle of solidified magma which underwent constant erosion from the lake's waters. Thus, the Fort looks like a steep-walled enclosure, while the Hole resembles a crater. Since the Hole exploded above the lake level, all its ash still forms a gradual slope away from the vent.

Both these quirks of Central Oregon geology are fun to explore together as one outing, especially in fall/winter/spring when the Cascades are snowed in.

Hole-In-The-Ground: From the west rim access point a steep trail plummets to the crater floor. There is a gentler .75m trail descending from the south rim. Hiking a loop down one trail then up the other takes about an hour. Notice the trees on the floor – check the needles and cones on these surprisingly located pines (page 130). The crater acts as a cold-air sink – at the bottom it's too cold for ponderosa seeds to germinate.

A rough dirt road circles the rim. It is pi miles long (remember geometry class? Circumference equals pi x diameter). For good views of the Cascades, Paulina Peak, and Fort Rock hike this road to its east rim highpoint.

Fort Rock: Picnic tables, bathrooms, and multiple infoboards surround a parking area. Tour the interior on an old roadbed. The western edge has bizarre rock shapes, easy-to-explore wave cuts, and a view over to the cave where Doc Cressman found the sandals (some of the oldest human relics ever found!)

Hole-in-the-Ground   Meteor Crater, Arizona

[DRIVE] From Bend take Hwy 97 south for 28m. Pass LaPine and near MP 169 turn left onto Hwy 31. Take this 22m and turn left onto gravel at signs for Hole. Set odometer and go 3m. You need to turn right onto dirt FS 3130 – sometimes there's a sign, but often it seems to disappear. Go one mile on 3130 to the rim access road. Leaving Hole, go left on 3130 for 1.5m. Turn right and go another mile to Hwy 31. Go left and at MP 29 turn left again at Fort Rock signs. Go 6m to town of Fort Rock, then left at Fort Rock park signs and 1.8m more to parking.

WHATEVER WHATEVER WHATEVER WHATEVER WHATEVER WHATEVER WHATEVER WHATEVER WHATEVER WHATEVER

Notice the bullet holes in the Fort Rock plaques. They were contributed by Charlton Heston's tireless N.R.A. volunteers.

An interesting video about Indian habitation in Central Oregon, including Fort Rock Cave, plays at the Lava Lands Visitor Center.

Lake/Resort/Eagles and Kokanee

14
- Drive Time from Bend: 90 min
- Total Outing Time Guess: 6 hrs
- Fee: free
- Dogs: leash
- Bathroom: yes

Odell Lake Wildlife

Simply the most unique wildlife spectacle in Central Oregon! In late Oct. and Nov. Odell Lake's abundant kokanee salmon spawn along the western shoreline and in the tributary rivers. Red 12-inch spawners color every nook and cranny. Few people come to see this, but plenty of bald eagles do. In Oregon, most fish are spawned out and dead by Nov. first, but not at Odell Lake. The run here lasts longer, attracting eagles from afar for a frenzied feast.

Shelter Cove Resort.

Jim and Trula Kielblock, owners of the Shelter Cove Resort, estimate that over 200 Bald eagles swarmed the lake in 2003! Their resort is the center of the action as eagles perch on the trees above their waterfront. Swooping down among the docks they grab big flapping kokanee and fly to the treetops to feed. Beware – they love to drop the leftovers on unsuspecting tourists!

The drive from Bend is about an hour and a half, but this excursion is so worth it. The beautiful kokanee are magic themselves, and a chance to see our national bird swoop and snag one just feet away from you is breathtaking and unforgettable!

Eagle-eye view.

For kokanee spawn info, see entry 52.

[DETAILS] Shelter Cove Resort is busy with fishermen all summer. There is plentiful camping and a bunch of rental cabins (about $30 per person/night). The spawn is quiet – few except birdwatchers are in the know. Call 541-433-2548 for details, reservations, road/weather conditions. The eagles feed primarily at dawn and dusk, but midday you'll see plenty soaring and cavorting.

Staying at the Shelter Cove Resort is best. Get there by 3PM for the dusk feeding and wake early to witness the morning frenzy. Spend the day looking for kokanee or visiting Salt Creek Falls. If your timing is right and the eagles are putting on a show, this experience is one you'll be telling your friends about for a long time!

Posing like on the back of a quarter.
Photo by Jim Kielblock

Note: Huge Salt Creek Falls (2nd highest in Oregon), is just 5m west of lake on Hwy 58.

Lakeshore trail littered with carcasses.

[DRIVE] Two ways to get there depending on early snowfall – each takes about 1.5 hours. If open, the best route by far is the Casc Lks Hwy. From Bend it's a gorgeous 70m drive, past Wickiup and Davis, to the Crescent Cutoff. Go right 4m then right again onto Hwy 58 for 10m to Odell West access, then 2m to resort.

If it's snowy, take Hwy 97 south 45m to Crescent then turn right (in the middle of town) onto the Cutoff. Follow it, then Hwy 58, for 22m to Odell West access.

Biologists guess that there were approximately 1,000 pairs of bald eagles in Oregon around 1800. By the 1960's only about 400 pairs existed in the *entire lower 48 states* (due to both hunting and DDT). Nowadays the estimate is about 6,000 pairs in the lower 48, thanks to the Endangered Species Act.

Scenic Hike/Drive-to Viewpoint/Waterfalls

15

- Drive Time from Bend: 15 min
- Total Outing Time Guess: 1 hr (view)
  3.5 hrs (hike)
- Trails: easy short/mod 4m one-way
- Fee: NW Pass
- Dogs: yes
- Bathroom: yes

Tumalo Falls

97 feet of awesome! The cover of this guide shows Tumalo Creek leaping off a basalt escarpment into a rainbowed basin. The viewpoint is mere steps from the parking lot or take a short trail to the top-o-the-falls fenced platforms. The top is a must – totally worth the 5-minute walk! Sure-footed adventurers might find a slippery path under the escarpment leading to a groovy red-rock nook behind the waterfall.

Tumalo Falls.

Happy Rebecca traverses snow into Happy Valley (late June).

There are multiple trail options from the parking lot, all are well-signed. Best by far though is the trail upstream along Tumalo Creek. Go just a mile to check out some more excellent falls or keep going a total of 4m to find Happy Valley. The valley's happy and you'll be happy too – it's a moderate trail of plentiful waterfalls leading to musical meadows spangled with wildflowers …yum. Tis possible to loop back via the Bridge Creek trail, but the Bend Watershed property is restricted and less scenic. Better to retrace your steps and enjoy all the sights and sounds of fantastic Tumalo Creek from the reverse angle.

Twin Falls picnic viewpoint.

HIKE Begin up to the falls then past. Trail passes Twin Falls in one mile then Upper Falls a mile further. Cross a footbridge and pass more falls before intersecting with the Bridge Creek trail at mile 3.7. Go straight .3m more to Happy Valley and its sunny meadows – the mapboard is your turnaround point. It's also possible to loop on the newer "Farewell Trail", but this trail caters mostly to mtn bikers because the Tumalo Creek trail is off-limits for downhill. Once again, the best route down is the Creek trail.

Lots of trails to explore at Tumalo Falls. Mapboard at trailhead is good and all trails are well-signed. Do something different every visit!

DRIVE In Bend, at the "Phoenix Rising" roundabout on 14th and Galveston, go west on Galveston. In 10m the road turns to gravel as it crosses the creek. Go straight for 2.4 washboardy miles to the parking lot.

WHATEVER WHATEVER WHATEVER WHATEVER WHATEVER WHATEVER WHATEVER WHATEVER WHATEVER

Bend is a rare town that does not have to filter its drinking water. Bridge Creek Watershed (Bend's supply) is so pure that it is only treated with a small amount of chlorine to ensure its potability. Hiking elsewhere helps keep it pure.

Mt. Bachelor

...kes/Mtn Views/Summer Chairlift/Restaurant

- Drive Time from Bend: 24 min
- Total Outing Time Guess: 2.5 (lift)
  3.5 (summit hike)
- Trails: mod/diff hikes
- Fee: free
- Dogs: yes
- Bathroom: yes

Map p.135

Bachelor Butte, at 9,065 feet, is the youngest of the major Cascade stratovolcanoes – only about 15-20,000 years old. Its symmetric cone escaped most of the Ice-Age glaciation that gnawed at the much older Sisters and Broken Top. This "Butte" became a "Mount" when the "Mt. Bachelor" ski area began development in the late 50's.

The original trail to the summit begins at the Sunrise lift and switchbacks arduously for 2.25 miles. The summit's 360-degree view is a delight worthy of the trudge – Cascade Mtns, Cascade lakes, and a whole lotta Bend overall!

Another popular, and less taxing, way to visit Bachelor (in July and August) is to take the lift from the west village to the Pine Marten Lodge. It costs $11 for adults, less for kids. The restaurant's views, while not as 360-ish, are still a whole lotta Cascades. A bit of a secret is that there is **No Charge** to ride the lift down – Woohoo, free! Thus, if you hike up to the lodge or over from the summit trail, you save $11 and get a free lift ride down. Tired legs love cold beers, warm decks, and free lift rides!

Happy hikers on the summit in September.

HIKE Here are two options from the west village that include the free ride down – check the ski-area map to get your bearings.

First, simply levitate up to the lodge via the service road – about 1.75m and 1400 feet. From the lift's base walk uphill to the dirt road at the bottom of superpipe. Go right on road and switchback up. At the red cinder hill stay sharp left. At "Thunderbird" sign go straight under lift then right and up. About 50 min. for fit folk.

Second: For a unique route to the peak and then over to the Pine Marten Lodge, climb the "West Village Getback" ski run for one steep mile to the Summit chair (where you'll pick up the summit trail). Head up from the chairlift base a bit and you'll see a dirt road angling up and

Chillin' on the NW lift.

left, at about a 10 o'clock angle into the trees. This is the Getback – follow it to the Summit chair, pass the chairlift building, and continue up and left to find the trail on the treed ridge. Now it's about 1.25m to the top. Coming down to this same point, now take the "Summit Crossover" road left and up, passing the Skyliner lift (about .75m and a 500-foot gain to the lodge). Your legs won't like more uphill at this point, but making a loop that includes lunch, drinks, and a chairlift ride is worth it!

DRIVE From Bend take the Casc. Lks Hwy for 18m. Sunrise lift is at MP 21, west village is at MP 22.

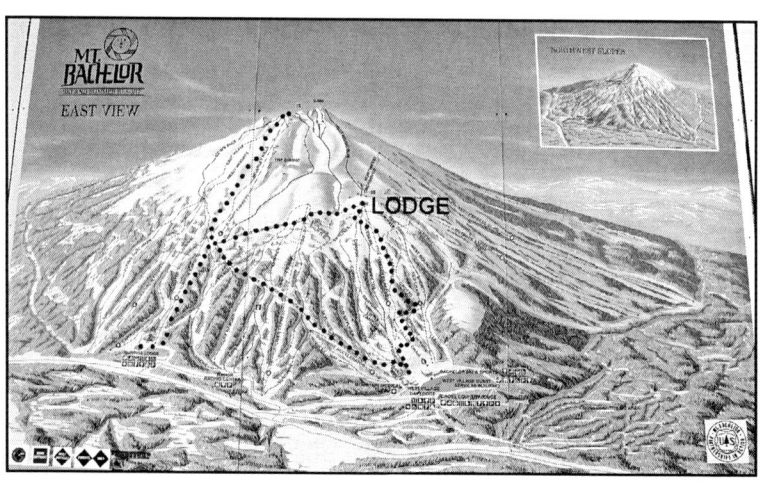

WHATEVER WHATEVER WHATEVER WHATEVER WHATEVER WHATEVER WHATEVER WHATEVER WHATEVER

The hill on Bachelor's north flank, right of the Summit Chart in photos, is the often mistaken cinder cone - similar to the one at west village. Nope, it's actually the terminal moraine that was left over from Batch's only significant glaciation.

Scenic Hike/Mtn Views

17

- Drive Time from Bend: 23 min
- Total Outing Time Guess: 2.5 hrs
- Trails: mod/diff 1.75m one-way
- Fee: NW Pass
- Dogs: yes
- Bathroom: yes

Map p.135

Tumalo Mountain

Hurry up – a fast driver and a fit hiker can make it from Bend to the top of Tumalo Mtn. in an hour! Try it – from 6,400 feet to 7,775 feet in 1.75m. This trail, while steep, is a joy. Hiked either for workout or pleasure, the views from the top are still wicked good. The Bendite fitness-nut, heartrate-monitored, low-carb spandex set may race up after work, but a slower pace will let your senses dance. As the trail ascends dense hemlock/lodgepole yields to spacious whitebark pine/subalpine fir. Steepening to the top, wildflowers reign, then whoa, the 360-degree vista is whammopano! Aside from the entire Cascade splendor, notice the recovering 1979 Bridge Creek Burn to the NE on Tumalo Creek (entry 15). Hey, is that the tip of Jefferson poking over Tam McArthur Rim to the north? Also, trace the Deschutes from the backside of Bachelor (Little Lava Lake), past Crane Prairie and Wickiup and then along the Lava Butte lava flows.

This trail kicks ass – the nearest trail to Bend where you get stellar views with a healthy workout!

A bikini top, a carrot top, and a Broken Top.

Nearing the summit.

DRIVE From Bend take the Casc Lks Hwy 18m. Past MP 21 turn right into Dutchman Sno-park to the far-end trailhead.

HIKE Up, down. No surprises.

WHATEVER WHATEVER WHATEVER WHATEVER WHATEVER WHATEVER WHATEVER WHATEVER WHATEVER WHATEVER

"Gala" means milk in Greek. Thus, the starry band in the night sky – our galaxy – became nicknamed "The Milky Way".

Scenic Hike/Mtn Views/Lake

18

- Drive Time from Bend: 25 min
- Total Outing Time Guess: 1.5 hrs
- Trails: easy 1.25 m lakeshore loop/diff ridge climb
- Fee: NW Pass
- Dogs: leash 7/1-10/1
- Bathroom: yes

Map p.135

Todd Lake

Quiet. Scenically book-ended between Broken Top and Bachelor. Todd, the nearest to Bend of the Cascade Lakes, is very popular with hikers, swimmers, picnickers, and campers. No boat ramp means no motors, but the short path from the parking area makes it easy to carry in your canoe, kayak, or raft. Weekends are usually very busy but there's plenty of room to spread out. Picnic tables are close enough to haul coolers and BBQs for a holiday bash.

Dog owners – the leash law is very strictly enforced here!

Campers – walk-in sites are free and first-come first-serve along the left side of the lake.

Swimmers – families with kids enjoy the far end of lake where bottom is gravelly and shallow.

Niki was hot, so Mike got her wet.

DRIVE From Bend take the Casc Lks Hwy for 20 miles. Just past Bachelor at MP 23 turn right onto signed access road.

Bachelor rising over the lake, taken from the ridge.

HIKE An easy 1.25m lakeshore trail takes about 30 minutes to circle the lake at a family pace.

A more rugged option is off-trail up the steep 500-foot ridge in front of Broken Top. It only takes 10-15 minutes to climb and the view of Bachelor sweetens every step. Atop the ridge go left and climb a bit more to an open spot where a postcard view awaits of Broken Top (9,175 ft) and Sisters (10,358/10,047/10,085). Impressive and totally worth the sweat!

Trailhead signboard/map details other hiking options.

A "moraine" is a ridge of glacially deposited rocks. A moraine lake forms behind a terminal moraine – the endpoint of the glacier's advance. Suttle Lake formed from an Ice Age glacier (roughly 10,000 years ago), whereas the smaller moraine lakes at Broken Top, T-F Jack, N. Sister, and Chambers/ Carver Lakes all formed in the 1920s at the end of a 500-year neo-glacial mini Ice Age.

Scenic Hike/Mtn Views/Lake

19

- Drive Time from Bend: 45 min
- Total Outing Time Guess: 4.5 hrs
- Trails: mod 6.5m o/b, mod 8m loop
- Fee: NW Pass
- Dogs: leash
- Bathroom: no

Map p.135

Broken Top

A symphonic journey of sight and sound to an area where the Forest Service inexplicably doesn't maintain a trail. Wide-open far-ranging vistas. Colorful stratification of BT's glaciated interior. Musical Soda Creek tumbling trailside. Crackling glacial ice calving into a green moraine lake. And topping the final ridge, jaws drop as eight volcanic exclamations line up in proud display. Describing everything could take pages. Maybe the Forest Service does know best – leave it unmarked so explorers and discoverers can ramble off-trail to find their own eye-candy nuggets.

HIKE An 8m loop is possible from the Crater Ditch trailhead, or a simpler 6.5m O/B starts from the BT trailhead.

For the Crater Ditch loop (ditch was built in 1914-15 to divert water into Tumalo Creek for irrigation, rather than letting it flow to Sparks Lake) hike along ditch for .75m until you come to the flood-ravaged wooden remnants marking the joining of

Four sisters in repose.

Soda Creek. Cross creek and hike overland up the left side of Soda. Pass the BT trail (heading to Green Lakes) and, for now, head towards BT's right shoulder. As slope steepens head right and go up and over a rock-strewn saddle. Once over you'll pick up the un-maintained trail to the lake.

Now, heading down to complete loop, stay with trail beside tumbling Soda Creek for 2.5m. Hop creek then turn right at the wilderness sign "trail" (straight here goes .5m to BT trailhead). On the trail re-cross creek and cruise a mile to Crater Ditch. Cross ditch and go left on the bank for 1.3m back to car.

For BT trailhead O/B, pass sign-in and go .5m to wilderness "trail" sign. Go straight onto unmaintained trail, cross creek, and continue about 2.5m to lake (directions above).

(DRIVE) From Bend take the Casc Lks Hwy 20m. Turn right at MP 23 to Todd Lake. Check odometer here. In .5m pass Todd as road roughens. Follow this 2.5m more, skirting meadows then up to plains. On the plains, with a clear view of BT, take a left onto FS 378 and go .5m along ditch to trailhead sign.

For BT trailhead, pass FS 378 and bump 1.5m more, making a left onto FS 380 (at BT sign) to dead-end parking.

OHMIGODWOW

Before hiking, drive to the Sparks Lake campground and read the sign detailing the 1966 cataclysm at BT's glacier lake and Soda Creek. Worth the 10-minute sidetrack.

Scenic Hike/Mtn views/Lake

20

- Drive Time from Bend: 27 min
- Total Outing Time Guess: 1.5 hrs
- Trails: easy 1m loop
- Fee: NW Pass
- Dogs: yes
- Bathroom: yes

Map p.135

Sparks Lake

The most scenic of all the Cascade Lakes! A photographer's dream and a favorite of Ray Atkeson, Oregon's late Photographer Laureate. You'll see scenes from this lake used in brochures, magazines, photos, and paintings allover Bend. The rugged shoreline with its basalt sculpturing and flowering nooks and crannies makes perfect foreground framing for the S. Sister/Devils Garden/Broken Top panorama!

An actual left-behind top.

Sparks is super shallow – great for families with venturesome kids or explorers with kayaks or canoes. Nobody really comes to fish, so there's not much hubbub. The lake extends surprisingly far to the south – about a mile. This arm, far from the Hwy, boatramp, and most everything, is delightfully serene and private.

There is nook, cove, island, or beach for everyone – even topless raft girls with one-eyed dogs! (Whew, guidebook photography is tough work!)

Maybe the dog is winking.

DRIVE From Bend take the Casc Lks Hwy 22m. Pass Todd Lake and at MP25 turn left at Sparks sign. Left at fork 1.5m to boatramp parking.

Atkeson trail postcard view.

HIKE Near the boatramp check out the Atkeson Memorial trail. A sign details the easy loop; it features a .25m paved wheelchair section contouring the photogenic shore and a cut thru the peculiar Davis Canyon. Totally worth a half-hour stroll (the first half is better than the second if time is tight).

WHATEVER WHATEVER WHATEVER WHATEVER WHATEVER WHATEVER WHATEVER WHATEVER WHATEVER

Sandy and Sasha were in town from Eugene for the Ben Harper concert (8/19/03). A local clued them in that Sparks Lake would be the primo place to explore with their raft while ridding themselves of their unwanted tan lines. Everyone's happy!

Scenic Hike/Mtn Views/Waterfalls/Lakes

21
- Drive Time from Bend: 28 min
- Total Outing Time Guess: 4.5 hrs
- Trails: mod 4.5m-6m one way
- Fee: NW Pass
- Dogs: leash
- Bathroom: Yes

Map p.135

Green Lakes Trail

If you ask around Bend, you'll find that this is everyone's "favorite" trail. The moderate 4.5m trail to the three Green Lakes offers plenty of waterfalls, lavas, and wildflowers as it gradually climbs alongside Fall Creek. It also offers plenty of company – this is definitely the most crowded trail in the Three Sisters Wilderness!

Trailside falls.

The Green Lakes basin is spectacularly nestled between Sister Charity and Broken Top. A waterfall on Charity's lava flow roars for exploration. The trio of lakes gives people lots of room to spread out, but since the lakes are too cold for swimming and dogs have to be leashed at all times…some think it's not too fun just to hang out.

Backpackers have loved lakeshore sites overly much. Restrictions have been put in place to ease over-use and spread people out. The concept behind "Wilderness" is to give both people and animals a chance at solitude in a natural, untrammeled environment. Because of its popularity, the Green Lakes Trail is failing as "Wilderness".

DRIVE From Bend take the Casc Lks Hwy 23m. Past Sparks Lake, at MP 26, turn right into signed parking.

HIKE Past sign-in, over bridge, then up along creek. Moraine Lake's junction comes at the 1.75m mark. Soon rock-hop across the lava-spring creek (curious may investigate its source), then over the Fall Creek footbridge. It's about 2 more miles to the Greenies. At the Park Meadows sign the main trail goes right then left. Circling all the lakes takes about 3m from this point. Tis possible to loop back to the car from here via Cayuse Crater/ Soda Creek, but this guide would rather Bend Over backwards to get you to try anywhere else than give any more options from this blitzed trailhead. Sorry/you're welcome.

Happy campers trekking past Green Lake and South Sister.

WHATEVER WHATEVER WHATEVER WHATEVER WHATEVER WHATEVER WHATEVER WHATEVER WHATEVER

In Central Oregon permits are needed to use the Obsidian Trail (entry 32) and Pamelia Lake (Mt. Jefferson Wilderness). Proxy Falls, Green Lakes, and S. Sister Climbers trail are all way overcrowded. The Forest Service doesn't want to place restrictions on use, but they are charged with preserving the Wilderness. How can you help?

Lake/Explorations

22
- Drive Time from Bend: 30 min
- Total Outing Time Guess: 2.5 hrs
- Trails: easy/diff hikes & explorations
- Fee: NW Pass
- Dogs: yes
- Bathroom: yes

Map p.134

Devils Lake

Devils Lake, a heavenly spring-fed pool of mesmerizing green waters, is too often just a quick stop for tourists or convenient parking for S. Sister climbers. Too bad for them. Don't overlook the charms of this lake! An exquisite day can be had exploring this area – bring an empty memory card plus a bit of enthusiasm and you'll surely get plenty of exorcise!

Idle hands at the Devil's sign.

Lakeshore trail "666" is the only maintained trail. It's an easy .5m stroll providing lots of eye candy – verdant forest and emerald water framed by the black dactite lava flow called "Devil's Garden".

There are also some little-known off-trail excursions leading to other film-devouringly beautiful spots. The lake's crystalline waters come from two sources: Hell spring and Tyee spring. Both springs inspire sighs as they gush forth from hillsides like fountains of moss! Each is no more than a half-mile from the lake. At the other end of the lake adventurous hikers can try a loop up and around the lower half of Devils Garden. This rugged overland jaunt sports good views, mysterious springs, rock inscriptions, Indian pictographs, and Devils Lake's hidden outflow – Satan Creek. A helluva trek!

Inscriptions.

A fountain of moss.

EXPLORE

Hell Spring. From the lot bathroom, follow the S. Sis climbers trail. Cross the Hwy then up. You'll be near the creek for a few minutes and as the trail swings left, listen for gurgle and head off-trail to the right and follow the creek to its spring. Takes about 10 minutes.

Tyee Spring. Harder to find but, like a Mounds Bar, "indescribably delicious"! The spring is about .5m from the parking lot and there are two options to find it. First, head up the

Elk/Devils trail. In about 12 minutes listen for water softly gurgling from your right. Head off-trail to the right here, hop a small stream and continue shortly to larger Tyee Creek. Scramble to its source. Or, from parking, begin on the S. Sis trail, cross the log bridge, and turn left up Tyee Creek. Clamber over Hwy and find the abandoned roadway heading up the right bank. This formerly was the 1960's trailhead road. Where it hits the creek was the parking and bridge to the Mirror Lakes trail. Don't cross the creek, but rather stay high on the right bank (careful not to cause erosion) and enjoy the pretty creek for about 10 minutes to its source.

Devils Garden. About a 1.5 hour loop, including a tough 600 ft climb. From the base of the flow at the Hwy, begin climbing next to the lava on the left. In around 15 minutes, you'll descend into a gully then up to an obvious saddle – notice some banana-like western white pinecones. This saddle is the top – trying to loop higher is possible, but a bitch. For killer mtn. views scurry up the dactite on the right. Continuing, cross the saddle and head down. Springs and streams play hide 'n' seek with you until you get to the flats where inscriptions decorate/deface the boulders. Finally, hop Satan Creek and up to the Hwy... Wait, do Bend's wonders never cease? On this last slope, curious eyes will find an array of faded Indian pictographs. Needless to say, be respectful of these rare treasures!

Up and around Devils Garden.

DRIVE From Bend take the Casc Lks Hwy for 25 m. Pass the lake and at MP 28 turn left and down to bottom lot.

WHATEVER WHATEVER WHATEVER WHATEVER WHATEVER WHATEVER WHATEVER WHATEVER WHATEVER

Lust, Sloth, Wrath, Envy, Gluttony, Pride, Greed

Sisters Mirror Lakes Loop

Scenic Hike/Mtn views/Lakes

23
- Drive Time from Bend: 30 min
- Total Outing Time Guess: 3.5 hrs
- Trails: mod 7m loop
- Fee: NW Pass
- Dogs: yes
- Bathroom: Yes

Map p.134

A scenic and fun 7 mile loop featuring S. Sis views, Wickiup Plains, LeConte crater, and then the swimmable Mirror Lakes. This moderate loop begins at Devils Lake and only gains about 600 feet the whole way. An extra short pant up the side of LeConte crater may or may not surprise you with a charming micro crater lake (late July/early Aug is the best bet). Even without the lake, the view over the Rock Mesa pumice/obsidian flow is dazzling! Next up is a whole basin of lakes. Sisters Mirror gets the name fame, but neighbors Bounty, Denude, and Lancelot are deeper rock-rimmed gems primed for diving, floating, and sunning. Bring whatever suits your style, bathing or birthday, cuz there's plenty of privacy, seclusion, and smaller lakes to be found off the beaten path!

DRIVE From Bend take the Casc Lks Hwy for 25m. Pass Devils Lake and then at MP 28 turn left and down to bottom lot.

Sister Charity spies the author in Denude.

LeConte's lake and South Sister

HIKE From Devils lot begin on the Elk/Devils trail. Thru underpass then .75m to first junction. Go right to Sis Mirror. In another .75m comes the Wickiup Plains junction, where the loop part starts. Go right. Emerging onto plains, Le Conte is the grassy hill to the left of Charity. Go left at the Moraine Lake junction (entry 24). Nearing crater scramble off-trail to its rim (attempting to minimize any erosion). Back on the trail it soon meets the PCT. Go left, the next 1.5m bringing you back into the forest, then right at the next sign to the Nash Lake junction. At Nash sign go straight and come to a quick fork. Left is PCT to Sis Mirror and beyond. For adventure go right, pass Sis Mirror and .25m more until you bonk into Bounty Lake. Left leads to large Denude, right leads to pretty rock-walled Lancelot. To go back, find the PCT on the shore of Sis Mirror, head straight thru Nash sign then right to complete loop back to Devils (Map shows another possible loop using the Nash trail, but it's long and dull).

Wickiup, LeConte, Rock Mesa, and Sisters.

The Three Sisters, as the story goes, were originally named, Mt. Faith (North), Mt. Hope (Middle), and Mt. Charity by the Methodist missionaries of Salem in the 1840's. Biblically, Paul the Apostle speaks of the virtues faith, hope and charity in Corinthians 13:13.

Scenic Hike/Mtn Views/Lake

24

- Drive Time from Bend: 30 min
- Total Outing Time Guess: 3.5 hrs
- Trails: mod 5-8m loop
- Fee: NW Pass
- Dogs: leash
- Bathroom: yes

Map p.134

Rock Mesa/Moraine Lk Tr.

This moderate 4.5m loop features side-visits to an interesting crater, a pumice/obsidian flow, and a turquoise moraine lake (all add considerably to the length of this hike). You do this by hooking together the Sis. Mirror Lakes trail with the S. Sis. Climbers trail from Devils Lake parking. The trail starts towards LeConte Crater then turns right from the Wickiup Plains to Moraine Lake. On the way you can venture into the pumiceous jumble of Rock Mesa via an abandoned US Pumice Co. road that snakes about a mile into the flow. Then, before descending, make a visit to popular Moraine Lake for a swim and an exploration of the secluded cascades that sometimes pour from the lake. This hike is very scenic and usually uncrowded until you get to over-used Moraine Lake. On weekends skip the lake unless you like plenty of company.

Rock Mesa's access below South Sister.

HIKE Begin by following directions to LeConte Crater in entry 23. After the crater backtrack to the junction and begin a 1.5m climb towards Moraine Lake junction. Be alert – in about .75m there are a couple of level stretches with clear views of S. Sister rising over Rock Mesa. At the second of these, notice the definite road-cut angling up and right in the distant lava wall. To check out this bizarre lavascape, head overland to the jumble, then up. The trail zigzags for a mile then abruptly ends – either backtrack or scramble down to the forest floor and back to the trail. Continue left to Moraine/ Sis. Climbers junction. A right turn here leads to the car, but first go straight .75m to Moraine Lake. Have a dip or venture along the right shore to scout for seasonal wildflowery waterfall wonderlands that may exist downstream of the outflow channel. Refreshed, backtrack to S. Sis. Climbers trail and descend steeply 1.75m to Devils Lake. Towards the end listen for Hell Spring gurgling to your left.

Hood River backpackers after a swim in Moraine.

DRIVE From Bend take the Casc Lks Hwy for 25m, turning left at MP 28 into Devils Lake lower parking area.

The US Pumice Co. exploratory road history: They filed a mining claim in the early 60's to extract pumice – before the 1964 Wilderness Act passed. When the company pursued the claim in the 70's there was a public uproar about the devastation that a new road, big mining trucks, and heavy equipment would cause to the pristine surroundings. Courts upheld the valid mining claim though, and necessitated Senators Packwood and Hatfield intervening to enact a two million dollar buy-out, which Pres. Reagan ok'd in 1982.

Scenic Hike/Mtn Views/Lakes

25

- Drive Time from Bend: 50 min
- Total Outing Time Guess: 4.0
- Trails: diff 2m one-way
- Fee: NW Pass
- Dogs: yes
- Bathroom: yes

Maps p.135 &140

Tam McArthur Rim

A semi-circle of 1,200-foot cliffs rise directly over two emerald-green lakes. A steep 2m trail climbs the 1,200 feet to the 7,732-foot prow on Tam's Rim where sightlines sweep from Bachelor to Hood. A triumphant view! The

The ridge past the rim.

Three Creeks Lakes glisten below like two olives in a fancy martini glass awaiting a toast. Eye-candy galore of the Three Sisters country! Enjoy the views then head down to one of the lakes for a dip before heading home.

The big lake is the most popular because of its rowboat rentals, drive-up shoreline, campsites, and beaches. For a bit more privacy pack your Camelbak cooler for the half-mile trek to the neighbor lakes. Warm waters invite skinny-dippin' in the shadow of the rim. No better day than a sunny hike with friends followed by frolic and tanning in one of Little Three Creek's nooks….mmmm.

Tracey overlooks the prow and Three Creeks Lake.

HIKE Rim trailhead is opposite Driftwood Camp entrance, at the lake's outflow. Begin with a steep 1m gasp. Some flat then another .5m up to the first rimpoint. The jutting prow to the left is your destination. The trail braids a bit, but all trails lead about a mile across the pumice slopes to the point.

Venturesome and energetic hikers can continue west past the prow. The trail fades at a snowfield, but keep going overland a half-mile to the western rim and ooh-la-la views. Scramble another rugged mile around the Broken Hand outcropping and you'll feast your eyes on Broken Top's watery treasures! (entry 19) Head back the way you came.

Once down, to find Little Three Creek lake either take a 1m signed trail from the Driftwood entrance or take a .5m unsigned, but obvious, trail from the endpoint of the campground road.

The rim rising over Lil' 3 Creeks Lake.

DRIVE From the center of Sisters turn south onto Elm St./FS 16. Follow it 13.7m on pavement, then 1.7m more on gravel following signs straight ahead for the lake.

We the people of the United States, in order to form a more perfect union, establish justice, insure domestic tranquility, provide for the common defense, promote the general welfare, and secure the blessings of liberty to ourselves and our posterity, do ordain and establish this constitution for the United States of America.

– Preamble to the Constitution, 1787

Scenic Hike/Waterfalls

26

- Drive Time from Bend: 60 min
- Total Outing Time Guess: 3.5 hrs
- Trails: mod .75m or 1.5m one-way
- Fee: free
- Dogs: yes
- Bathroom: no

Map p.140

Squaw Creek Falls

One for diehard waterfall lovers only, because the road to get here is a bitch. (If you just want a waterfall that's big, easy, and wow, go to Proxy (entry 35) or Sahalie (36) instead – they both take about the same drivetime and are much easier on the nerves and car.)

Squaw Creek Falls gets the publicity on this hike because it's located just an easy .75m jaunt from the trailhead, through a nicely pine-scented forest. But, arriving at the falls, the viewpoint is disappointing weak sauce. You've got to be able to athletically scramble down the loose, unmaintained slope to get to the base of the falls. Only at this misty creekside do you get to see Squaw's surprisingly triangular form. Scamper over the wet logs into the mist on a sunny day and you'll have a rainbow encircle you – sweet!

Note: only crazed adventure monkeys try to sneak behind the falls to the mossy grotto.

Venturesome waterfall lovers need to keep hiking upstream on a faint, unmaintained .5m user-trail. Grandeur awaits! You'll pick your way along the left side of the creek for about 15 min until…Zow – a few hundred feet of cascading creek dubbed "the Cascades". Very Yosemitesque!

Note: only insane waterfall lovers would cross the creek and scramble to the big boulder's flatish top to make love. Why? Cuz the Black Butte lookout might see you.

Creekside mist.

Cascades from the boulder.

DRIVE Only 14.5m from Sisters, but the washboard and gnarly dirt are so slow it takes about 35 min – OK for most cars though. From Sisters' center turn south on Elm St. and go 7m. Turn right onto washboard FS 1514. Rattle 4.8m and look for FS 600 just before Squaw bridge. Turn left onto 600 and follow it 2 rough miles until it ends at FS 680. Go left on 680 for .3m to trailhead.

HIKE .75 miles to overlook. Creek scramble is down and right. Cascades trail is up and left.

WHATEVER WHATEVER WHATEVER WHATEVER WHATEVER WHATEVER WHATEVER WHATEVER WHATEVER WHATEVER

Oregon Senate Bill 488 (in 2001) outlawed the word "squaw" for place names in Oregon. Other states have done the same because, to Native Americans, "squaw" is a vulgar and insulting term for female genitalia. The Forest Service is charged with renaming Squaw Creek as well as all other "squaw" locales.

EVER WHATEVER WHATEVER WHATEVER WHATEVER WHATEVER WHATEVER WHATEVER WHATEVER WHATEVER

Scenic Hike/Mtn Views/Glacier Lake

27

- Drive Time from Bend: 43 min
- Total Outing Time Guess: 6.0 hrs
- Trails: diff 5m one-way
- Fee: NW Pass
- Dogs: yes
- Bathroom: yes

Map p.137

N. Sister - Thayer Glacier Lake

A FABLE:

Once upon a time the Three Sisters, Faith, Hope, and Charity danced gaily together on a warm spring day. As they twirled, Hope playfully grabbed and pulled aside Faith's snowy white robe. "Gee," giggled Hope, "What colorfully striped undies you're wearing!" Shocked, Faith quickly

Up Soap Creek to the moraine under Faith.

reached to cover her exposed backside. Over her shoulder though, she caught sight of randy old Broken Top and his young buddy Bachelor leering at her behind. Feeling embarrassed, yet somewhat flirty with her new striped underwear, Faith fancied that she'd flash them a bit more to really make their glaciers melt! Alas though, she was caught. Mother Nature, who was treating Old Man Mazama for heartburn a bit to the south, spied her and flew overland in a rage. "How dare you taunt the boys and set such a bad example for your younger sisters," Mother demanded. "I'll have to teach you a lesson...." Mother decreed that every autumn until the next glacial advance, Faith would have to sit in a cold glacial puddle with her robe pulled aside for all to see her colorfully striped underwear. "Let that be a lesson!"

Faith now sits shamed, but secretly she's a bit proud. Broken Top and Bachelor got so hot that they barely have any glacial cover themselves! And, slowly, Faith has collected rocks around her so her undies are difficult to see unless you're adventurous. She knows a new Ice Age will come soon to cover her...until then she waits... The End.

If you love rarely seen beauty, try this trek. The whole hike is gorgeous, but you won't believe the 2,400 feet of colorful stratovolcanic innards towering over the glacial lake!

DRIVE From Sisters, take Hwy 242 west for 1.3m. Turn left onto FS 15 and go 11 washboardy miles, following signs for Pole Creek Trailhead.

HIKE 5m one-way from Pole Creek to Thayer Glacier. From Pole Creek sign-in head thru the beetle-kilt pines for 1.25m. At Green Lakes junction stay left, then .75m more to Soap Creek. 100 yards before Soap Creek look for the unmaintained climber's trail heading upstream. Follow this trail 1.75m as it ascends next to the creek. As the trail crests a steep, open ridge, Faith towers to the left. Leave the trail here and head left overland towards the bouldery moraine slope left of the large yellow rock outcropping. Reaching a meadow chock-full-o' stream channels, scramble up the slope to the notch in the moraine and...!!!

Icebergs and stripes.

WHATEVER WHATEVER WHATEVER WHATEVER WHATEVER WHATEVER WHATEVER WHATEVER WHATEVER WHATEVER

Bend is not located where it is by happenstance. Bend's location is the only easily crossable section of the Deschutes for miles in either direction. From the Old Mill to First St. rapids the Deschutes flows at ground level. Both up and downstream sheer basalt walls impound the river. The Indians forded the river at Bend, as did the early pioneers with their livestock. Settlers heading west crossed the Deschutes and bid its last bend farewell. Thus "Farewell Bend" was born, later becoming just Bend.

Skylight Cave

Cave exploration

28
- Drive Time from Bend: 40 min
- Total Outing Time Guess: 2.5 hrs
- Closed 11/1 - 4/15
- Fee: free
- Dogs: no
- Bathroom: no

Spend a May/June morning in this cave and you'll witness a glorious sunlight-show! Three "skylight" holes in the roof of this lava tube let three beams of sunlight shine down to the cave floor. The wet cave floor steams where the beams hit it. The steam plus airborn dust highlights the sun-streaks for an ethereal display! Wake up early though cuz our planet  rotates fast – the spectacle only lasts from about 9AM to 11AM. Throughout the summer the beams still show up a little, but only in the spring does combination of the moisture and sun angle dazzle.

Like most other local lava tubes there is a ladder descending into the opening. The skylights are left about 200 feet over rough terrain. To the right the cave extends approx. 700 feet. This section has some breakdown and stoopways where you'll have to duckwalk a bit, but the rewards are great keyhole-shaped passages.

The cave is closed *from Nov. 1 thru April 15* for bat habitat protection. Please honor this closure so that this cave isn't fenced (like some others have been). Sunbeams don't work in the winter anyhow.

DRIVE From Sisters head west on Hwy 242 for 7m. Just past MP 85 turn right onto red-cinder FS 1028. Follow 1028 3.8m until you see "Dry Creek Trailhead" intersection. Go straight but turn right quickly onto red-cindered spur 260. Follow this .7m – it turns to rougher dirt just before the righthand maybe-signed cave entrance.

EXPLORE Use cave smarts: lantern, flashlight, lighter, solid shoes, warm clothes, functioning brain. People whose brains don't function should wait outside and shoot their guns.

A modest cave bare.

WHATEVER WHATEVER WHATEVER WHATEVER WHATEVER WHATEVER WHATEVER WHATEVER WHATEVER WHATEVER

For goddess-like sunbeam photos of your girlfriend: you need a tripod, no flash, shutter open for about a half-second, and a patient goddess-like girlfriend.

Scenic Hike/Mtn Views

29

- Drive Time from Bend: 36 min
- Total Outing Time Guess: 5.0 hrs
- Trails: diff 3.75m one-way
- Fee: free
- Dogs: yes
- Bathroom: no

Map p.137

Black Crater Trail

A strenuous and steep 3.75m trail climbs 2400 feet to this red-cindered peak. A great trail for someone looking for a sweaty workout, a lousy choice for someone wanting a moderate jaunt. The trail climbs steadily through the thick forest with minimal glimpses of the views to come. As you near the peak an array of wildflowers dots the slopes – blue lupine, red indian paintbrush, and orange-ish jester-hat columbine. Finally, amidst wind-tortured whitebark pines, the trail gains the summit and a panorama of snowy peaks unfolds! Reach out and touch Washington, marvel at Belknap's extensive lava flows, scope out some good-looking Sisters. Sharp eyes may spy Dee Wright and the tip of Bachelor.

Nearing the cindery summit.

Whitebark and Washington.

DRIVE From Sisters take Hwy 242 west for 11m. Pass Windy Pt. And at MP 81 turn left into signed trailhead parking.

HIKE Simple out 'n' back with no options.

EXTRA For adventurous folk, try to find the hidden lake that fills a steep-sided basin on B.C.'s east flank. Like other "secret" Cascade lakes it's warmish, it's fishable, it's secluded, and it's not listed in most guidebooks. Same here. But here's some tips for explorers: get a map and a rugged car and locate FS 790. At the highpoint of this road there is a short spur road. Find the ATV-wide trail off this spur and scurry about a half-mile to this nugget!

Happy girls and tired puppies among wildflowers.

Getting to know our bark beetles: Rice-sized female beetles bore into the bark of stressed pine trees. The tree will try to repel the attack by oozing pitch in an attempt to drown and expel the invaders. A weakened tree in an overburdened forest will not be able to repel the attack.

Eggs are then laid in a "gallery" between the bark and wood. As the larvae grow they tunnel through the wood and into the bark (leaving the rutted patterns you see on deadwood). Adult beetles eat an exit hole through the bark and fly off to attack another tree.

Look for pitch tubes, sometimes with a dead beetle stuck to it. Also, look for exit holes that look like BB holes.

Matthieu Lakes Trail

30 Scenic Hike/Mtn Views/Lakes

- Drive Time from Bend: 40 min
- Total Outing Time Guess: 3.5 hrs
- Trails: mod 6m loop
- Fee: NW Pass
- Dogs: yes
- Bathroom: yes

Map p.137

A quintessential Cascades trail! This moderate 6m loop highlights everything we love – epic mountain views, swimmable lakes, lava flows, high country trees, and bonus options. The route is friendly for most anyone – it joins the PCT and only gains about 700 feet the 3m to the south lake. On the way you'll be treated to a ridgetop vista of peaks lined up with North Matthieu Lake nestled below. Soon comes emerald little South Matthieu Lake with lavas and two Sisters framing its beauty – pretty enough for another local guidebook's cover!

Wash, Jack, Jeff, Hood from N. Lake's lava ridge.

If both lakes are busy, or you've just got lots of energy, you can continue past S. M. Lake for another downhill mile to search out a faint trail to "secret" Yapoah Lake. Though not as scenic, its off-the-beaten-path locale means few people on its sunny beach.

Hard to beat this hike. No long climbs, so bring a pack heavy with food and drinx to offer a toast to High Cascade splendor!

DRIVE From Sisters take Hwy 242 west for 14m. At MP 78 turn left to Lava Camp Lake/ PCT. In .3m turn right at sign for horse-use trailhead (Lava Camp Lake campsites are straight).

HIKE From the sign-in head right towards PCNST (Avoid the Millican Trail, it's viewless and boring). Fork left onto PCT then .5m to loop junction. Go left to S. M. Lake – 2.6m. The ridge views are 2m, then shortly to the N.M. Lake junction. First go straight for S.M. (For side trip to Yapoah, go left around S.M. to the Scott Pass trail. Descend Scott for about a mile. The faint, right, unsigned .3m spur to the lake is easy to miss – look sharp for a rockpile marker. If you begin up a slope, you've gone a little too far.) Back at the N.M. junction, cruise down .5m to N.M.Lake. Main trail goes right, but a primitive trail goes left around the lake and gives you a chance to climb a lava heap for a postcard view. Reconnecting with main trail follow it a mile down to the junction. Now go left then soon right, back to car.

North Sister over South Matthieu.

According to Tam McArthur: The Matthieu Lakes are named for Francis Xavier Matthieu, a pioneer of the Oregon country who aided in the establishment of the first Oregon provisional government in 1843.

Viewpoint/Scenic Hike

31

- Drive Time from Bend: 40 min
- Total Outing Time Guess: 2 hrs
- Trails: various
- Fee: free
- Dogs: yes
- Bathroom: yes

Map p.137

Dee Wright Observatory

The castle from the interpretive trail.

A fascinating respite amidst young and otherworldly lava flows atop McKenzie pass. Located on scenic Hwy. 242, first timers often stop and gape at the beauty of this scene. The "observatory" is a small castle-like room built around 1933 out of actual lava rock (by F.D.R's C.C.C.) It houses a compass and portals identifying all the surrounding Cascade peaks. Yup, this "observatory" will answer all those pesky "which mountain, how high, and how far away?" questions that any drive in our Cascades provokes.

Don't miss the .5m (15 minute) pathway beginning near the steps. It's an easy paved stroll thru some pretty cool lava terrain enlivened by a scad of info signs. Also, a pavilion near the castle details the human history of the area.

DRIVE From Sisters, take Hwy 242 west for 14m to M.P. 78.

HIKE Two options on the nearby P.C.T.:

First, just .5m west of Dee is the PCT north trailhead. Most guidebooks head you north from here for a 3-mile lava trek to little Belknap Crater – Bah, this is kind of boring!

The second option is to hike south on the PCT (from the less-obvious place where it crosses 242 just .2m west of Dee.) This section cruises thru the lava field for one mile with smashing views of North and Middle Sisters, then junctions and continues 1.5m to sparkling N. Matthieu Lake (Entry 30 for more). The variety here is sure to please – lava, views, and a swimmable lake...ooh la la!

Mtn. identifier.

Watching the B and B forest fire erupt from the observatory (Aug. 19, 2003)

WHATEVER WHATEVER WHATEVER WHATEVER WHATEVER WHATEVER WHATEVER WHATEVER WHATEVER WHATEVER

Belknap is a basalt "shield" volcano, topped by a cinder cone. Basalt, a very fluid lava, flows far from its vent, creating a broad cone, or shield – like the Hawaiian volcanoes. The Sisters are "composite" or "strato" volcanoes, built steeper by less fluid lavas such as andesite.

Scenic Hike/Mtn Views/Waterfall

32

- Drive Time from Bend: 51 min
- Total Outing Time Guess: 5.5 hrs
- Trails: diff 11m loop
- Fee: NW Pass
- Dogs: yes
- Bathroom: yes
- Permit req'd

Map p.136

Obsidian Trail

Sweeping views of North and Middle Sisters, alpine meadows dotted with springs and tarns, a 20-foot waterfall, and amazingly marbled obsidian – all in an 11m loop. The banded rhyolitic glass is everywhere at the top elevations – walls, gullies, boulders, hunks, and flakes – all colored with Mother Nature's fingerprints!

Alas though, the moderate elevation gain combined with the great visuals and rare obsidian has lead to overuse. Backpackers and PCT thru-hikers all seem to want to camp around the sensitive alpine meadow. Thus, a permit is required to either day-hike or backpack into the area. Call ahead to reserve one from the McKenzie Ranger Station – 541-822-3381. They can fax the permit to either the Bend or Sisters office for pick-up.

Despite its popularity, this trail is not the best one around. Half of its length is somewhat dull, the waterfall area is often crowded, and the permit planning is a pain. Unless you're an obsidian fanatic you may want to check a good guidebook for some less crowded options.

HIKE Past sign-in the trail meanders easily for 3m through hemlock forest. Contour up and into a lava flow for .5m (Collier Cone's flow which continues to Linton Lake and Proxy Falls). Hop across White Branch Creek to the trail fork

A tarn, a tent, and Sister Faith.

Icy Obsidian Falls.

that begins the loop. Start right to Linton Meadows. In the next 1.5m notice some obsidian hunks and the first of the three rock-mounted trailside plaques. Junction with the PCT and go left, arriving shortly at Obsidian Falls. Above the falls is the meadow where it's easy to spend an hour at the springs, ponds (tarns), and investigating the red-yellow-black whirly-swirly obsidian outcroppings. (J. Crew would describe them as sangria-camel-night.) Lots of mountain visuals the next mile of trail as it drops to a flowing creek and junction. Take a left onto "Glacier Way trail 4336" and descend .75m back to the loop junction. Go right, through lava again, then 3m back to car.

Note: Map shows Spring Lake at the end of a .5m spur about .5m from the trailhead. Looks inviting for a dip after a long hike, but No – it's spring-fed cold with muddy shores after a wicked-steep descent. Skip it.

DRIVE From Sisters take Hwy 242 west. Pass Dee Wright and down to MP 71. Just past Scott Lake turn left at signed road for trailhead.

Whirls and swirls.

Plaques for Bronaugh, Montague, and Prouty were placed early in the 1900's by the Mazamas Mountaineering Club to honor esteemed members.

Scenic Hike/Mtn Views/Lakes

33

- Drive Time from Bend: 50 min
- Total Outing Time Guess: 5 hrs
- Trails: mod 7.5m O/B or 9m loop
- Fee: NW Pass
- Dogs: yes
- Bathroom: yes

Map p.136

Tenas Lakes/Scott Mtn. Tr.

This hike is a piece of cake – beautiful Benson and Tenas Lakes are the cake and wildflowery Scott Mtn is the icing! Hard to make a better hike than this – an option for every desire.

Hoodoo, Hayrick and Hood huddle with Jeff and Jack.

Benson Lake comes first – a rock-rimmed basin of blue. A bit further are the Tenas Lakes, "Tenas" is Chinookan for "little" and there are about five of these green gems within a half-mile radius. Except for busy weekends you can usually find your own private lake for some secluded Cascade mega-sunshine. Past Tenas the trail climbs 6,116-foot Scott Mtn with its commanding view of... zow, western Cascade glory: hikes and hot springs, caves and canyons, lakes and lavas, waterfalls and wonders. Ahhh...soak up the sweeping views then head back for a soak in a lake...Paradise found!

DRIVE From Sisters take Hwy 242 west for 20 m. Pass Dee Wright then 5 more miles down to MP 72. Turn right at sign for Scott Lake and follow gravel one mile to dead-end trailhead parking.

HIKE Two options – 7.5m out/back or a 9m loop, both from the same parking.

Out/Back: Start on the Benson Lake trail, which leads 1.3m to an unsigned lakeside campsite (primitive trails explore the lake and ridge). Continue one mile to the signed spur to Tenas Lakes – left to the first lake with more lakes further west. For Scott Mtn go past Tenas .8m to a junction with an unsigned trail leading to the right (this is the loop connection). Go straight for a steep .5m to the top. Head back the same way.

Loop: Going counter clock is wise – start past Scott Lake, skirt Hand Lake, summit Scott, then return past Tenas and Benson for a dip. From parking start on the Hand Lake road/trail and soon skirt left around lil' Scott Lake. Trail narrows and goes about 1.5m to Hand Lake and its Belknap lavas. Next 1.5m contour lava flow (passing a pioneer lava-crossing road) until reaching a sign "Bunchgrass ridge/Hand Lake". TURN LEFT here onto the unsigned trail that climbs into the forest for 1.8m to the Scott Mtn junction. Climb Scott then descend and complete the loop past Tenas and Benson.

Scott Mountain above a Tenas Lake.

Life shrinks and expands in proportion to one's courage.

— Anais Nin

Scenic Hike/Lake/Waterfalls

34

- Drive Time from Bend: 59 min
- Total Outing Time Guess: 4 hrs
- Trails: mod 2m one-way w/diff scramble
- Fee: NW Pass
- Dogs: yes
- Bathroom: yes

Map p.136

Linton Lake/Falls

Waterfalls roar above a fish-filled lake surrounded by a majestic old-growth forest – sounds pretty damn good, huh?! Then why do some guidebooks bore you into skipping this one with tripe like, "hike moderately two miles past old-growth to chilly Linton Lake and its attendant falls" – hardly inspiring.

Here's what you get if you Bend Overall: To visit the best-kept secret off the McKenzie Hwy, find the steep scramble trail on the nearside of Linton Creek before it dumps into the lake. Why?? Because Linton Creek hurtles over this glacier-carved wall for nearly 1000 feet before pouring into the lake. Up this creek are an unsurpassed series of monstrous waterfalls, virtually unknown to the public, yet awaiting inspired adventurers! The first 80-foot falls is a mere 12-minute log-hopping scamper. Most folks would be satisfied and head back. Not You! Five minutes more of heavy breathing and you'll gasp "Wow" as the next stairstep torrent appears. Need more? There are more, but the path disintegrates into a steep, loose, and challenging grapple for the

Lava shoreline.

First stop – about 80-feet tall.

next 20 minutes – only for true connoisseurs of Cascade secrets.

Look for these falls in Greg Plumb's definitive "Northwest Waterfall Guide" – they aren't in it. Ask around, can you find anyone who knows they're here?

After your venture, back at the lake, open a beer and catch come rays. Imagine a hot Sept. day; waterfall serenading, vine maple coloring, chilly swimming, hot sunning, laughter echoing …ahhhh, a diem well carped!

Stop two – Wow!

DRIVE   From Sisters take Hwy 242 west for 26m over McKenzie pass. Continue down to MP 66 and the roadside pulloff for Alder Springs Camp and the adjacent Linton Lake trail.

HIKE   The Linton Lake trail leads 2m from Hwy 242 to the Obsidian Creek dead-end campsite. From here either rock-hop along the shore or find the faint trail leading to the Linton Creek campsite. The faint scramble trail heads straight up from this campsite.

WHATEVER WHATEVER WHATEVER WHATEVER WHATEVER WHATEVER WHATEVER WHATEVER WHATEVER

Lava has dammed this lake – it has no visible outlet. Lava flowed from N. Sister's Collier Cone and down this glacially-carved valley before blocking up this lake and then continuing to Proxy Falls. Go down to lava dam to see some of Linton's falls high above the lake.

Scenic Hike/Waterfalls

35

- Drive Time from Bend: 60 min
- Total Outing Time Guess: 3 hrs
- Trails: easy 1.25m loop
- Fee: NW Pass
- Dogs: yes
- Bathroom: yes

Map p.136

Proxy Falls

A super-popular 1.25m loop trail visits both Proxy waterfalls after touring a bit of lava and massive old-growth forest. This trail has a well-deserved reputation for ease and beauty, and thus it seems like everyone driving over McKenzie Pass stops for a half-hour jaunt. Avoid weekends – you can't even park!

Crowded or not, both waterfalls are beauties. Lower Falls, the first stop, cascades about 200 feet down a glacier-carved wall. Photographers often scramble down to the creek with their tripods for some idyllic framing. A second spur trail leads to Upper Falls. Shaped like a 100-foot stairway to a mossy heaven, these falls empty mysteriously into a pool with no visible outlet.

In mid-October the fall colors can be remarkable and the tourists with the kids are gone – talk about unrivaled Central Oregon beauty!

HIKE Signboard at the parking area details the 1.25m route.

DRIVE From Sisters take Hwy 242 west for 27m. Just past Alder Sprgs/ Linton Lake trailhead, at MP 65, slow down for roadside parking.

A forest pixie in her sylvan idyll.

Lower falls.

Ice-Age glaciers carved the walls of this canyon, leaving Lower Falls a 200-foot drop. Recently, geologically speaking, Collier Cone (next to N. Sis.) spewed lava which oozed 13m down this canyon, passing the Obsidian trail then damming up Linton Lake before stopping near Proxy Falls (check map 136,137).

Scenic Hike/Waterfalls/Drive-to viewpoints

36

- Drive Time from Bend: 60 min
- Total Outing Time Guess: 3 hrs
- Trails: mod .5 or 2.5m hikes
- Fee: free
- Dogs: leash
- Bathroom: yes

Sahalie/Koosah Falls

Sahalie Falls pavilion.

Possibly the prettiest riverside trail anywhere! Imagine two surging 80-foot waterfalls, a captivatingly turquoise river, old-growth forest, blankets of moss, and scattered lava flows. It's like having a bit of distilled New Zealand in our backyard!

There are two ways to experience the wonders on this stretch of the McKenzie River. Park at either waterfall and simply walk the easy half-mile trail between them, or, better yet, make a moderate 2.5m loop by going up one side of the river then down the other. In summer both waterfalls can be very busy because they are well-signed and just off the highway. For a little more adventure and seclusion hike the loop. The far bank feels remote – you probably won't even notice the throngs of people at the viewpoints, but if you do you'll be glad you're not one of them. The really v e n t u r e s o m e should look for the slippery path leading to the alcove behind Sahalie Falls – mist, moss, rainbows, and thunder await the brave!

The beauty of the upper McKenzie River is eye-boggling! It's celebrated in Oregon tourist brochures and even national advertising. This short section of aquamarine crystal-clarity, bookended between two thunderous waterfalls, is undoubtedly one of Oregon's finest exclamations!!

Sahalie Falls as pictured in an actual 1971 *Playboy* ad.

Koosah Falls.

DRIVE From Sisters take Hwy 20 west for 26m. Over Santiam Pass then stay left at the Hwy 20/22 junction. Three more miles then turn left onto Hwy 126 to Eugene. Pass Clear Lake and at MP 6 park either at more-crowded Sahalie or just past at Koosah.

HIKE Start at either waterfall parking and choose either upstream or downstream to begin. It's about 1.25m on each side. Upstream the trail passes Sahalie and arrives at a log bridge in .5m. Cross the bridge and head downstream passing Sahalie then Koosah. A few minutes past Koosah turn left on the spur trail signed "Carmen Res." The trail emerges at an outhouse – go left, over bridge then left again onto the upstream trail.

Holy!!! In July 1998 Shannon Carroll, a 20-year-old female kayaker, kayaked over 78-foot Sahalie Falls to set a world record (since surpassed). Whew, hard to believe!

Scenic Hike/Mtn Views/Lake/Resort

37

- Drive Time from Bend: 60 min
- Total Outing Time Guess: 4 hrs
- Trails: easy 4.5m loop
- Fee: free
- Dogs: yes
- Bathroom: yes

Clear Lake

Clear Lake is one of the numerous spring-fed lakes dotting the Cascades that features amazingly clear aquamarine water. Surprising though is Clear Lake's unique origin. Only about 3000 years ago local lava flows dammed both the inflow and outflow of a section of the McKenzie River. Water coursed through the lava, emerging as springs, creating Clear Lake. As the lake filled it drowned the surrounding forest then overspilled the dam, making a new "headwaters" for the McKenzie. The

Rental boats.

lake's waters are so cold and algae-free that the 3000-year-old drowned trees don't decay much, and today you can still see the submerged stumps near the north end of the lake (either via trail or boat).

This lake is popular and packed on summer weekends. Most people come to camp, boat, fish, and picnic though, leaving the lakeshore trail to pensive hikers or the occasional gung-ho mtn biker.

Clear Lake Resort: Cabins for rent, old-timey café/restaurant, some groceries/no booze, rowboat rentals. No phone – you just gotta go.

Crockett Lodge at Clear Lake Resort

HIKE An easy 4.5m trail circles the lake – a feast for the eyes! Start and finish either at the Resort or Coldwater Campground. Highlights are the awesome Great Springs, the drowned forest, the northern bench viewpoint (Three Sisters reflected in the lake), huge old-growth trees, lava flows, and scenic bridges. Plus, some of the prettiest blue water anywhere. This trail is unreal in October when the vine maples add their explosion of color!

The drowned forest.

Trailside view – the Sisters rising over the resort.

DRIVE From Sisters take Hwy 20 west for 25m over Santiam Pass. Stay left at the 20/22 junction then in 3m turn left onto Hwy 126 to Eugene. In 4m turn left at signed entrance to Resort. 35min Sis.

WHATEVER WHATEVER WHATEVER WHATEVER WHATEVER WHATEVER WHATEVER WHATEVER WHATEVER WHATEVER

Springs fill the lake year-round with 38-degree water. Lake doesn't freeze, but it doesn't warm up either. Only polar bares come to swim.

Undeveloped Caves

38

- Drive Time from Bend: 51 min
- Total Outing Time Guess: 2.5 hrs
- Fee: free
- Dogs: no
- Bathroom: no

Sawyers Caves

A group of short lava tubes sporting an interesting variety of features. Thousands of cars pass by these caves daily, but since the Forest Service "unsigned" them years ago, few people know to stop.

The two main caves are up and left from the parking area. In about 100 yards you'll find a big opening with a large skylight. This cave goes in about 300 feet over a rugged bottom surface.

Libby ponders the entrance skylight.

Octopus hunting.

Bring a lantern or multiple flashlights and a hat to protect your noggin from bumps. There's a breakdown section that you'll need to negotiate – if you've got enough light you'll see some reddish ropey "pahoehoe" lava, resembling redwood bark, and also a neat little side passage. Further, the cave opens again for easy walking over a floor featuring great swirls of ropey lava – maybe the best display of "pahoe-hoe" in any of Oregon's caves!

Past this first cave entrance a faint path continues into the forest. A big tube awaits in a few hundred yards with a land-bridge spanning the openings. The caves are jumbled and not that interesting, but the bridge is cool.

Finally, back at the parking area, down and right 100 feet, are two short tubes. The further one is eerie. You have to lower yourself into it then duckwalk. Thirty feet within it there appears to be a sleeping octopus. Be brave, go look!

Cave interior.

DRIVE From Sisters take Hwy 20 west 28m. After Santiam Pass stay left at the 20/22 split and check your odometer. Go 2.2m from the split. Slow down when you see the big yellow sign "Trucks: Length Restricted". The square parking area is on the left side across from this sign. If you get to Hwy 126, you've gone one mile too far.

WHATEVER WHATEVER WHATEVER WHATEVER WHATEVER WHATEVER WHATEVER WHATEVER WHATEVER WHATEVER

The eye has two types of cells for vision. Cones are for color and detail in daylight and rods are for black and white vision in low light. It takes the eye about 30 minutes to gradually adjust from cone vision to rod vision. Thus, when entering a dark cave with just a flashlight, your cones won't work in the dim light, but slowly your rods will activate and begin to "see" – though only in black and white with little detail. On the other hand, if you bring a bright lantern into the cave, your cones will still function and you'll be able to "see" the colors and details of the cave features. (Cont'd p. 93)

Scenic Hike/Mtn Views/Lake/Wildflowers

39

- Drive Time from Bend: 60 min
- Total Outing Time Guess: 5 hrs
- Trails: mod 4m loop w/extras
- Fee: NW Pass
- Dogs: yes
- Bathroom: yes

Map p.139

Canyon Creek Meadows

This loop hike is all about colors – colors that sound like ooh, ahh, and wow! From Jack Lake a moderate trail winds 2m to Canyon Creek Meadows – arguably the finest wildflower showcase in Central Oregon! But it's not only flowers that color this hike. Their rainbow array conspires with Three Finger's striped innards and glistening white glaciers to eat your film. Take a mile-long offshoot trail (past mid-Aug. when snows melt) which leads first to the upper meadows, then scrambles up a moraine slope. Wow, a little green lake at the glacier's foot is filled with snow and icebergs that melt to create Canyon Creek, while Jack's colorful turrets preside 1,800-feet overhead. Fantastic! Pre-2PM light is best for photos on east-facing Jack.

Loop junction.

B & B burnt trees around Jack Lake. May 2004.

Heading down to complete the loop you pass a small waterfall marking an optional .7m sidetrip to chilly blue Wasco Lake – a nice bonus jaunt.

Overall, this scenery's unforgettable! Tricky though is to time both the mid-summer wildflowers and the late-summer snow-free trail to the moraine lake. Better go twice – beauty this vibranbrant inspires devotion!

Note: The B&B fire raged thru this area. This trail has many burned areas, but no re-routing.

DRIVE From Sisters take Hwy 20 west for 11m. Near Mp 89 turn right onto Jack Lake Road (FS 12). Go 4.2m then left onto FS 1230. Go 1.6m, passing Jack Creek, then stay left onto gravel. One mile then stay left again onto FS 1234. Now bump-bump your way 5m to the lake trailhead.

HIKE From parking to lake then around sign to the right. Skirt lake then .3m to loop junction. Head left 1.75m to first meadow. The loop continues right, but the optional trail heads faintly left here, for a steep mile, to Jack's moraine lake. Retracing back to the loop, go left one mile to the waterfall/ Wasco Lake junction. Option .7m to lake or head straight 1.5m back to car.

Approaching Jack through the upper meadows.

WHATEVER WHATEVER WHATEVER WHATEVER WHATEVER WHATEVER WHATEVER WHATEVER WHATEVER

Rods and cones cont'd from Sawyers Caves…At night when you step outside to see the stars it takes time for your rod vision to activate (cones are at work inside the lighted house)… slowly you see more and more stars. The stars all appear white though because rod vision only sees in black and white. Each star actually has its own color, which a properly exposed photograph will reveal.

Scenic Hike/Spring-fed River

40
- Drive Time from Bend: 40 min
- Total Outing Time Guess: 2.5 hrs
- Trails: easy .5m/1m one-way
- Fee: NW Pass
- Dogs: yes
- Bathroom: yes

Head of the Jack

NW Pass parking.

The Head of the Jack is the area where a myriad of springs gurgle from a wooded hillside, accumulating into Jack Creek. A wide, flat half-mile trail leads to the springs and a short nature loop. The "Head" is a long time favorite for both locals and campers. Seemingly misplaced amongst old-growth ponderosa and Douglas fir, this mossy idyll soothes the soul. The Head of the Jack is a great place to screw around and get off. the trail – test your balance on the fallen trees or find a hollow one to crawl into Spring-fed creeks like this never really flood, so the downed trees and wildflower islands don't wash away. Moss is able to thrive abundantly everywhere along this chilly creek, softening the sounds of swishing grass and flowers…so nice!

A huge, campground (now $10) borders the creek downstream of the Head. Families with kids love the place because it's wide open for ball games, bike rides, frisbee, etc. Bring a milk crate to chill your drinks in the creek!

Jack Creek

Note: Head of the Jack was mostly unaffected by the B&B fire, other than some sporadic burnt areas. The only change is the new $10 camping fee.

Bridge over gurgled water.

HIKE There are two trailheads. The free one is at the far upriver end of the campground. It's a roadbed beginning at a big ponderosa then leading 1m along the creek to the Head. The other is the "official" trailhead that requires a NW Pass. It begins at a trailhead 1.5 dusty miles past the campground – then .5m to Head. But why drive an extra 1.5m and pay $5 to save only a half-mile walk. Not.

DRIVE From Sisters take Hwy 20 west for 12m. Near MP 89 turn right onto Jack Lake Road (FS 12). Go 4m then left onto paved FS 1230. In .7m cross creek and turn left onto FS 1232. Campground is immediate or follow signage to far trailhead.

> The B and B Complex wildfire began on 8/19/03 and burned 91,915 acres – the largest fire in Deschutes Nat'l Forest history. It was attributed to lightning strikes that smoldered for ten days before weather conditions ripened for an inferno.

Fish Hatchery/Scenic Hike

41
- Drive Time from Bend: 45 min
- Total Outing Time Guess: 2 hrs
  hike: 3.5 hrs
- Trails: easy 2m one-way
- Fee: free
- Dogs: yes/leash
- Bathroom: yes

Wizard Falls Hatchery/Metolius

Riddle me this Batman, "What kind of wizard died to create a hatchery?" Find out by spending a relaxing hour or two at this famous fish hatchery. Stroll the manicured grounds to see tanks of fingerlings and a pond of lunkers.

Feed the fish – pellet dispensers give a handful for a quarter and it's hard tellin' who's more frenzied, the fish or the kids feeding them! Interpretive signs, benches, and picnic tables complete the scene.

Ooh-la-la blue.

Two surprises: 1) A pair of bald eagles have nested on the ridge west of the hatchery for about ten years. Spy their ridgetop nest and look for them perched in the bare treetops. 2) The weirdest things ever are the two-headed Siamese trout kept in an indoor tub. Ask one of the friendly hatchery staffers for a quick peek at these shocking bizarros!

From the hatchery, riverside trails head both upstream and down along the crystalline Metolius. Learn about some fish, take a soothing walk beside the incomparable Metolius, take a picture from the bridge, have some lunch, and plan your next outing. Central Oregon can't be beat!

Just 25 cents.

DRIVE From Sisters take Hwy 20 west for 10m. Past MP 91 turn right onto FS 14. In 3m stay right, then 7m more to the signed left turn to the hatchery.

HIKE The Metolius River Trail. A great 2.5m section of the river trail heads upstream from the hatchery along the west bank. This section is many peoples' favorite because it stays near the river with no private property, detours, roads, nor campgrounds. This stretch ends at Canyon Creek Campground, but a good turnaround point is at the two-mile mark where an 80-foot-long spring pours into the deep blue river – Gorgeous! Before hiking everyone should walk onto the bridge at the hatchery to gaze and photo the most magically aquamarine spot on this river's short (30 mile) run to Lake Billy Chinook.

Frenzied feeders from Black Butte Ranch.

Elevations in feet:
Bend 3623   LaPine 4280   Sunriver 4165
Redmond 2985   Sisters 3165   McKenzie Bridge 1400
Madras 2242   Prineville 2864

Viewpoint/Mtn Views/Famed Spring

42
- Drive Time from Bend: 35 min
- Total Outing Time Guess: 1.5 hrs
- Trails: easy, short paved path
- Fee: free
- Dogs: leash
- Bathroom: yes

Head of the Metolius

As picturesque as Central Oregon gets! Sit listening to the Metolius springs gush…gaze flowing with the river past orange ponderosas and verdant meadows…then rising to the snow-capped peak of Mt. Jefferson.

A perfectly framed scene, but few photos truly capture the sense of beauty and tranquility. Take them anyway.

An easy quarter-mile paved pathway leads from a picnic area to the fenced viewpoint above the springs. First-timers crinkle their brows in puzzlement at the fully formed river sprouting from the dry hillside. Old-timers know that the waters travel under Black Butte from the Black Butte Ranch swamp (swamp sits 300 feet higher than the springs). Kids love the cute squirrels begging for handouts.

For most people this is about a half-hour stop on the way to the hatchery or a hike, or a last stop before driving back to the Willamette Valley.

The head of the trail.

The Head of the Metolius.

Note: In September kokanee salmon migrate upriver to spawn. Check entry 52 for details.

DRIVE From Sisters take Hwy 20 west for 10m. At MP 90 turn right onto FS 14 (Metolius Camps). Go 4m, staying right at fork, to signed entrance.

WHATEVER WHATEVER WHATEVER WHATEVER WHATEVER WHATEVER WHATEVER WHATEVER WHATEVER WHATEVER

The springs gush about 50,000 gallons per minute – that's the equivalent of about five gasoline-tanker truckloads.

Scenic Hike/Mtn Views

43

- Drive Time from Bend: 44 min
- Total Outing Time Guess: 4 hrs
- Trails: diff 2m one-way
- Fee: NW Pass
- Dogs: yes
- Bathroom: yes

Black Butte Trail

A lone, proud sentinel standing aloof to the east of its High Cascade relatives, wise old Black Butte was often mistaken for a young cinder cone because of its conical symmetry. But no – paleomagnetic dating surprised scientists by revealing a million-year-old composite volcano! Black Butte, feet planted in the bed of the ancient Metolius River, watched all the surrounding

Carol, Elizabeth and a poodle named Harley.

peaks arise as perfect cones like his own, only to be ravaged by Ice-Age glaciers into their current craggy forms. Not Black Butte – he stands in their rain shadow, suffering no glaciers. Surprised he is, though, when looking down he sees that the Metolius has found its way underneath him, reappearing as a gushing spring. Damn!

Black Butte.

Hard to find a better place to appreciate Central Oregon geography than atop this 6,436-foot butte. The 2m trail is fairy steep and sustained (gaining 1,600 feet) but the summit rewards are worth every gasp! View peaks from Broken Top to Mt. Adams. Tour the existing 1995 lookout tower, the antique

1924 "Cupola" lookout structure, and the debris from the 84-foot 1934 tower (collapsed in a winter storm, 12-7-01). Bring a map and binocs. Spy Suttle Lake and Hoodoo Ski Area. How 'bout Smith's Monkey/Burma and far to the SE, Paulina Peak. Straight down to the north look for the Head of the Metolius and its distinctive meadow. Then, over on the south side, look down to Black Butte Ranch where the Metolius' waters originate in the swamp. Plan for about an hour at the top – it's that good!

DRIVE From Sisters take Hwy 20 west for 5.4m. Turn right onto FS 11 – Indian Ford Camp. Go 3.7m then turn left onto gravel FS 1110 and follow it 5 winding miles to the trailhead dead-end.

HIKE Straightforward 2m climb with no options. 30 steps into the trail look up to see the tower on the summit.

The Cupola lookout and Harley, Jefferson.

Paleomagnetic Dating: Molten rocks often contain iron-oxide indicators which align to the earth's magnetic field at the time of their solidification. The earth last reversed its polarity 780,000 years ago – from pointing south to pointing north. Black Butte's oxides surprisingly point south, indicating its ancient age. All oxides in the other High Cascade peaks point north!

Scenic Hike/River Canyon

44

- Drive Time from Bend: 41 min
- Total Outing Time Guess: 3.5 hrs
- Trails: mod 1.5 or 3m one-ways
- Fee: free
- Dogs: yes
- Bathroom: no
- Closed 12/1 thru 4/1

Alder Springs Trail

Wade across Squaw to a many-springed meadow.

Hike from juniper desert to a lush creekside nestled under colorfully layered canyon walls. A moderate 1.5m trail descends into the fabulous geology of Squaw Creek canyon, passing Alder Springs on the way down. All the weird rock shapes and layering are "The Deschutes Formation" – 7 million years of volcanic ash and debris interbedded with river sediments. Kind of like a mini Grand Canyon! At the creek, de-shoe for a slosh through the foot-deep creek to a grassy picnic area/turnaround point.

Or, better yet, keep going. An unmaintained trail goes downstream another 1.5m to the Deschutes River con-fluence. Deluxe accommodations include a jutting prow of layered rock and a massive stand of ponderosas. Hot-summer-day heaven! If the solitary beauty of the rivers/rocks/trees doesn't scream at you to remove your sweaty clothing, take a quick dip, then sun-dry on the smooth rocks under the scented pine trees... well, if it doesn't then return this guide for a refund and move to Cleveland!

(DRIVE) From Bend take Hwy 20 west towards Sisters for 10.5m. About a mile past the roadside viewpoint

The confluence rocks!

turn right on Fryrear Rd. Go 5.5m to Hwy 126/Holmes Rd. (From Sisters take Hwy126 east 5m, from Redmond take Hwy126 west 13m). Cross 126 onto Holmes and follow it to MP 7. Exactly at MP 7 turn left onto gravel FS 6360. Go thru gate, leaving it as found, then 4m (watch odometer) to Alder Springs sign. Turn right for .7m rough road to trailhead.

Guardian hoodoos.

(HIKE) Pass comment box then quickly to Old Bridge junction (side trip here is short, but only so-so). Go straight along rim and drop a mile into Squaw Canyon. At the steeps listen and notice Alder Springs on your left while the bizarre pillars stand guard to the right. Cross creek to find the campsite lunch spot. Frolicksome nature lovers will find the trail on the lefthand side of the creek that leads 1.5m down to the confluence. Strip, dip, bask, smile, laugh, kiss, and repeat! Back the way you came.

WHATEVER WHATEVER WHATEVER WHATEVER WHATEVER WHATEVER WHATEVER WHATEVER WHATEVER

"If we keep on. We could go to Oregon. I heard there's human beings there . . ."
— **George Hayduke to Bonnie Abbzug in Ed Abbey's** *The Monkey Wrench Gang* **(Chap. 20).**

Petersen Rock Gardens

Renowned Rock Sculptures

45
- Drive Time from Bend: 11 min
- Total Outing Time Guess: 1.5 hrs
- Open: 9-5 365 days
- Fee: $3 (donation)
- Dogs: leash
- Bathroom: yes

A quirky testament to one man's passion for Central Oregon's rocks. Rasmus Petersen collected and sculpted this 4-acre wonderland throughout the 1930's and 40's. It garnered international acclaim: castles of obsidian, bridges of petrified wood, and walkways of wonderstone – all intertwined with ponds and canals full of lilypads and bullfrogs.

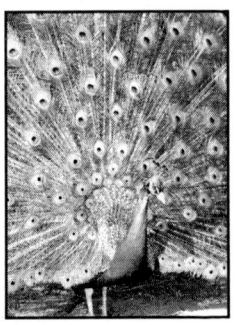

This place is one-of-a-kind! Peacocks in full plumage and odd-colored roosters strut amongst a carved Statue of Liberty and an American Flag mosaic (count the stars for a history quiz). The sampling of melted-lava tree molds are rare – you'll never see a better collection than these!

Petersen Rock Gardens is an original Central Oregon tourist destination, and everyone should still visit! Bring a picnic, kids, and the parents – the kids will run about, play, and search for a souvenir feather, giving you a chance to puzzle over the enormous task Rasmus undertook to assemble this oddity.

Lilies, bridges, and Lady Liberty.

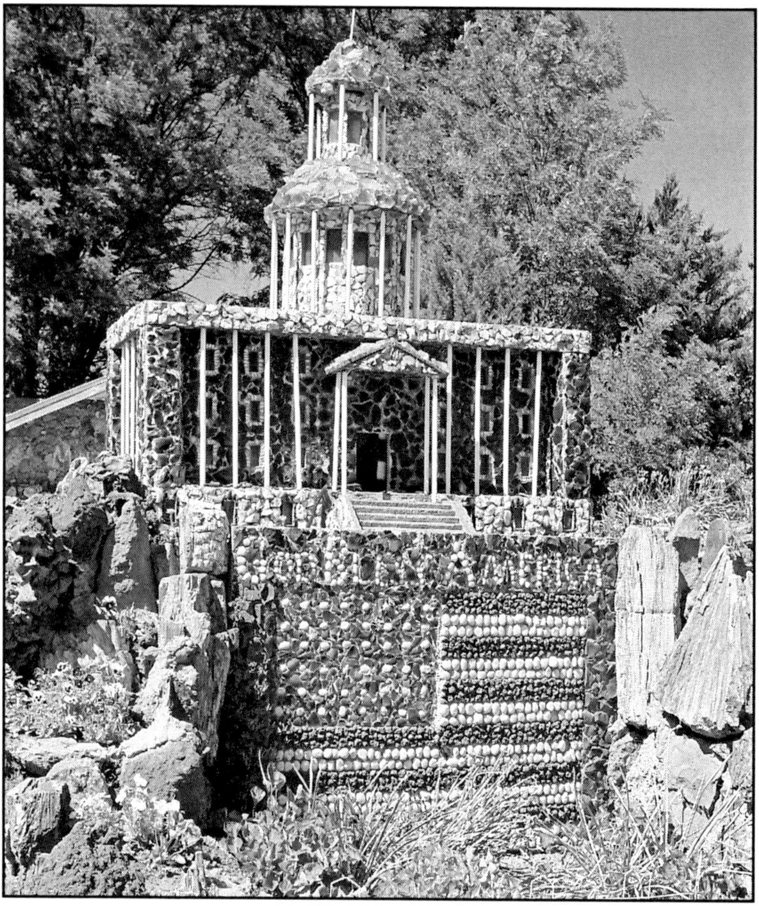

Flag mosaic.

DRIVE From Bend take Hwy 97 north 6.3m. At Petersen signs turn left onto Gift road then immediately right. Go one mile then left onto Young road. Straight one mile, crossing intersection, then right onto 77th for .5m to entrance.

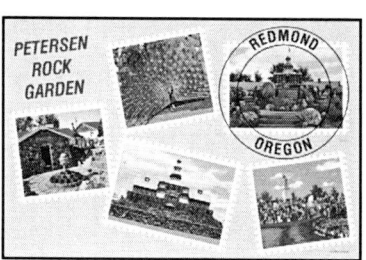

WHATEVER WHATEVER WHATEVER WHATEVER WHATEVER WHATEVER WHATEVER WHATEVER WHATEVER WHATEVER

Alaska admitted 1958, Hawaii 1959. Remember "Hawaii 5-0"? The "5-0" represents the 50th state. "Book 'em, Danno!"

WHATEVER WHATEVER WHATEVER WHATEVER WHATEVER WHATEVER WHATEVER WHATEVER WHATEVER WHATEVER

Smith Rock State Park

Scenic Hikes/Mtn Views/Rock-climbing Mecca

46
- Drive Time from Bend: 28 min
- Total Outing Time Guess: 3 hrs
- Trails: easy/mod/diff
- Fee: $3 State Park fee
- Dogs: leash
- Bathroom: yes

This park features an epic panorama of unexpected beauty – colorful 700-foot walls rising directly above the meandering Crooked River. Something for everyone: celebrated photogenic beauty, world-class rock-climbing, scenic hiking, picnicking, mtn bike trails, horse trails, camping, and lots of wildlife (golden eagles, deer, beavers, herons, river otters, and even a monkey!) Smith Rock is one of Oregon's premier state parks. If you can't find something to enjoy at Smith, you should just quit living!

Climbers: Get a guide at either Redpoint in Terrebonne or at Juniper Junction on the entrance road. No detailed route beta is available inside the park.

Mtn Bikers: Map detailing bike-use trails is free at the pay station. Better in-depth descriptions are available in local bike guidebooks. An epic ride is up Burma road, around Grey Butte, then looping back past Monkey Face.

Camping: Tent-only sites off the entrance road are $4, showers $2. Most regulars head for the free BLM "Skull Hollow" site – It's 10 min from the park (leave the park and go left left for 2m to a stop. Go left for .7m, then left again onto Lone Pine Road. Now 4m to the signed camp.)

Climbers on Morning Glory wall.

DRIVE From Bend take Hwy 97 north for 21m, passing through Redmond. About 4m past Redmond you come to Terrebonne. At the yellow traffic light turn right onto B Ave. Go .5m then left onto First St. Go 2m and look for the small entrance sign.

HIKE Easy trails are on the bluff or down and along river. The Misery Ridge/Monkey Face trail is a popular Mod/Diff 1.5m out 'n' back or 3m loop. Burma Road/Monkey Face trail is a less-used Diff 6m loop.

Misery/Monkey Trail: Definitely one of the most scenic hikes in Oregon – the grandeur of rocks, river and Cascades! From the rim head down and across the footbridge. Go straight to begin the .75m "most difficult" climb to Misery Ridge. Once atop, head right. At first glimpse of the monkey's head, the trail turns right for a steep .5m descent – careful, it's way loose. At the monkey's base go sharply right down to the riverside trail. Now head left for an easy 2m cruise around all the rocks and climbers back to the footbridge.

Burma/Monkey loop trail: (Note, map shows that this trail does not connect, but it does via an un-maintained scramble trail). Start down and across footbridge then right along river. Look for beaver-gnawed juniper and cliffside eagle nests. It's an easy mile to the trail register/ litter. Go left, steeply up to and around canal, then up Burma Rd. Reaching the top of the Burma saddle…gaze far! Road goes straight to Grey Butte, but for this loop, go left down the trail. At the dip fork right onto the singletrack and follow this loose trail for 1.2m as it contours behind the ridge. There are no signs marking the many short spur trails. Eventually you need to take a right fork that crosses a hillside to a Monkey Face/river viewpoint notch. From here the unmaintained steep, loose, switchbacky trail plummets .3m to meet the riverside trail. Two options from here. The easy way is to follow the river trail upstream for 2m back to the footbridge. The hard way is to head up towards Monkey Face to climb the steep trail to Misery Ridge and then down to the footbridge (only 1.25m this way, but a tough climb for tired legs).

Trailhead view.

WHO IS JOHN GALT? WHO IS JOHN GALT? WHO IS JOHN GALT? WHO IS JOHN GALT? WHO IS JOHN GALT?
Ayn Rand

River Canyon/Waterfall/Swimming Hole

47

- Drive Time from Bend: 43 min
- Total Outing Time Guess: 3 hrs
- Trails: steep .5m one-way
- Fee: free
- Dogs: yes
- Bathroom: yes

Steelhead Falls

No flowery adjective-riddled guidebook rah-rah needed here…just…This Place is Killer! Best damn swimming hole around! Deschutes canyon. 12-foot waterfall. Towering striped walls. 15-25 foot diving rocks. Huge deep pool. Hot Sun. Steep half-mile trail.

Go on a 100-degree day to jump, play, sun, and drink with the locals, or go anytime else year-round for remarkable scenery and solitude. Explore at least a mile downstream on a fishermen's trail.

Psyching up.

Whitey hucks it!

DRIVE Complex directions, but it only takes about 15 minutes from Terrebonne. From Bend take Hwy 97 north 22m to Terrebonne. Pass small T'bonne and a half-mile to the north turn left onto Lower Bridge Road (signed Crooked River Ranch). In 2m turn right onto NW 43rd then 1.8m to a T. Go left on Chinook for one mile then left into Badger. Follow Badger (becomes Blacktail) for 1.6m to its end at Quail. Turn right onto gravel for one mile then left onto River for the final mile descending to the trailhead.

WHATEVER WHATEVER WHATEVER WHATEVER WHATEVER WHATEVER WHATEVER WHATEVER WHATEVER

The masonry walls left of the falls are the remains of a 1922 fish ladder built to help the fish in low flow years. Round Butte Damn, built around 1964, wiped out virtually all the namesake Steelhead – but sharp eyes may still see a jumper in the fall.

Boating/Fishing/Scenic Hike/Mtn Views/Lake

48
- Drive Time from Bend: 42 min
- Total Outing Time Guess: 5 hrs
- Trails: mod 6m loop
- Fee: $3 State Park fee
- Dogs: leash
- Bathroom: yes

Lake Billy Chinook

Rim drive viewpoint.

This man-made reservoir was created in 1964 when the Round Butte Dam backed-up the combined flows of the Deschutes, Crooked, and Metolius Rivers. Today Billy Chinook represents many things to many different users. Beauty-lovers liken it to a mini Lake Powell – a desert oasis enclosed by spectacular basalt walls. Fishermen love it as a premier kokanee lake. Water-skiers can always find glassy water. Camping is plentiful. And, on hot summer weekends, the party is on! More rednecks than a Wal-mart – speedboats, jetskis, bikinis, and drinkin' hold sway. Bring your own cruising vessel or rent one at the marina (houseboats also – a popular idea for crazy bachelor/bachelorette parties).

One of Central Oregon's most distinctive geologic features are a

Balanced rocks.

Deschutes Formation Palisades.

bunch of balanced rocks on a hillside overlooking the Metolius arm. Erosion of the Deschutes formation has left tapered pillars topped with flat capstones. These rocks are well-known to locals, but kept sort of secret by the Forest Service until measures could be implemented to protect them from vandalism. Thus, new for 2004, the roads to the rocks have been obliterated and the veil of secrecy loosened. You must now hike in .2m to see them – no more tailgate parties raining the rocks with beer bottles and shotgun shells.

It's a long drive to see them. From the Deschutes crossing bridge, continue up then zig zag west another 12m. Drop into Fly Canyon and as you rise out of it, back onto gravel, look for a small right-hand pullout just past FS 1170. Park and walk in. Please – just look, don't climb.

HIKE The Tam-a-Lau is a 6m loop beginning with a steep mile to the plateau top. In summer it sees a lot of use, but in the off-seasons the solitude is complete. Excellent views of the "Deschutes Formation" strata, the snowy Cascade peaks, and a shining blue lake impounded by sheer basalt walls. The trailhead is 4m from the marina, adjacent to the "Upper Deschutes Boatramp" entrance.

DRIVE From Bend take Hwy 97 north for 34m. Past the Crooked River bridge, on the downslope of the next hill, turn left at signs for Cove Palisades State Park. Go 2m into Culver then left for a few miles of signed zigzags until descending to the lake.

WHATEVER WHATEVER WHATEVER WHATEVER WHATEVER WHATEVER WHATEVER WHATEVER WHATEVER WHATEVER

Basalt lava often cools into two distinct forms. The top of the flow, exposed to the air, cools rapidly into a jumbled mass called "entablature." The lower layers, insulated by the top, cool slowly and form six-sided columns called "columnar." The alternating layers of columnar and entablature are formed from successive flows often thousands of years apart.

Self-serve Thundereggs/Exotic Rock Shop

49
- Drive Time from Bend: 60 min
- Total Outing Time Guess: 4 hrs
- Open: 7am-5pm 365 days
- Fee: free
- Dogs: yes at dig only
- Bathroom: yes

Richardson's Rec. Ranch

Unusual and one-of-a-kind! Indian legend has it that angry spirits bombed each other with thundereggs. Richardson's specializes in these tennis-ball sized agate-filled "bombs" which have held the distinction of Oregon's State Rock since 1965. This low-key ranch caters to both "rockhound" collectors and families with curious kids. This is no snobby showroom gig – Johnnie and Norma's humor keeps this a fun and playful mom, pop, kids, and grandkids operation – amazingly open every single day for the past 30 years!

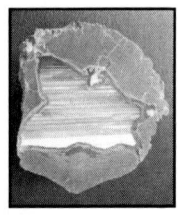

Old-timey charm at the shop.

There are at least three great reasons for a visit. First, the shop's displays of polished rocks, geodes, fossils, spheres and thundereggs are dazzling. Second, the yard outside is jumbled with heaps of exotic rocks for sale or just curiosity. Third, hunt for your own unique egg. Norma will loan you a pick, bucket, and a map so you can drive the 6m to the various eggbeds. It's easy pickins – just dig a bit in the "loosened" beds and you'll find a bunch! Each egg costs about fifty cents and the shop will cut it in half for about another buck. Wow, everyone gets a one-of-a-kind souvenir for only about $1.50 – that's bang for the buck! If you don't want to spend an hour or two drivin' and diggin', then simply pick one off the shop's pile to have cut.

Summers are busy and fun and sometimes hectic on holidays—digging and cutting non-stop. Around November rain closes the road to the beds until March. The shop stays open but cutting is sporadic in the off-season when the kids are in school.

Inside the shop with $15 of just-cut eggs.

DETAILS

- Phone 541-475-2680 for info and cutting schedule.
- Free camping and showers on the grounds.
- 6 mile, 20 minute dirt drive to beds.
- The shop will cut any rock you bring from home for 25 cents/inch.

DRIVE From Bend take Hwy 97 north for 40m to Madras. Go through Madras and at the north side of town head right on Hwy 97 towards The Dalles (straight is Hwy 26 to Portland). Go 11m and watch for signs for Richardsons at MP 81. Turn right, go 1.8m, then right again onto gravel for the last mile to the ranch.

WHATEVER WHATEVER WHATEVER WHATEVER WHATEVER WHATEVER WHATEVER WHATEVER WHATEVER WHATEVER

The "Recreational" in the name is from the old days when they offered sport hunting and horseback rides.

Scenic Hike/Wildlife Oasis/Mtn Views

50
- Drive Time from Bend: 46 min
- Total Outing Time Guess: 2.5 hrs
- Trails: easy 1.5m loop
- Fee: free
- Dogs: leash
- Bathroom: yes

Rimrock Springs Trail

Paved path to the first platform.

Grab your binoculars for this chock-full-'o'-wildlife High Desert wetland oasis. An easy 1.5m loop trail begins with a half-mile paved wheelchair/stroller section leading to the first viewing platform. Ducks quack, hawks soar, beavers slap, birds chirp…and the deer and the antelope play. Seldom is heard a discouraging word from the birdwatchers who flock to Rimrock Springs! Past the platform the trail becomes dirt but still very easy-going. It quickly leads to the second viewplatform – a highlight because of its peculiar array of beaver-felled junipers. Take a faint trail from this platform about 100 yards to see some incredible 12 to 24-inch diameter trees that the beavers chewed but left standing. These Oregon beavers were dam busy!

Backtracking from this viewpoint, the trail then slopes up to the "rim". When the skies are not cloudy all day, the vista sweeps from Bachelor to Hood.

Unlike the dramatic scenery of Smith Rock, this place is low-key. Rarely any visitors. Go for a quiet, reflective stroll and keep your eyes peeled fer some critters.

Unfinished beaver business.

DRIVE   Located on Hwy 26 between Madras and Prineville. From Madras go south on Hwy 97 and quickly turn left onto Hwy 26. Go 10m then left into signed parking area. From Terrebonne or Smith Rock check Driving tour 3 on page 124 for directions.

"Home On the Range" was written in 1871 by Dr. Brewster Hisely about his Kansas home.

Scenic Hike/Geologic Curiosity

51
- Drive Time from Bend: 60 min
- Total Outing Time Guess: 4 hrs
- Trails: mod 2m one-way
- Fee: free
- Dogs: yes
- Bathroom: no

Stein's Pillar Trail

This 44 million-year-old pillar towers as a Central Oregon geologic icon! A bit like Smith Rock's Monkey Face, but Stein's Pillar is …hard to describe. Standing erect, this member of the rhyolite family pokes 350 feet skyward from a wooded hillside. Historic fallacy has lead to discoverer Enoch Steen being misspelled as "Stein".

There are two ways to see this peculiar monster. A drive-up viewpoint with an interpretive sign is located on Mill Creek Road. But the viewpoint doesn't do justice to the pillar's size. For an up-close perspective there is a 2m trail that rambles through an incredible forest to the pillar's base. Whoa, the enormity is daunting! Sit in the overhang/cave and munch a lunch as you gaze north over the Mill Creek Wilderness. Look for the 1800's inscription and imagine the courage it took to make the first ascent to the top in 1950.

From the viewpoint.

HIKE From the NE corner of the parking loop the unsigned trail begins faintly then soon crosses a streambed. For the next 2m the trail contours hillsides before reaching the rock outcrop viewpoint. From here descend some steep forest stairs to the base of the pillar.

Mill Creek flowing below.

DRIVE About a 50m, one-hour trip from Bend. Take Hwy 97 north to Redmond then turn right onto Hwy 126 east to Prineville (19m). Intersect with Hwy 126 and continue east thru Prineville. In about 8m you'll pass Ochoco Reservoir. At the far end look for MP 28 and turn left onto Mill Creek road. Go 5 paved miles then straight on gravel another 1.7m to trailhead turnoff – FS 500. (Go straight here 1.3m to roadside viewpoint). For trailhead turn right and check odometer. Cross bridge and climb 2.0m to a turnaround loop on the left – this is the trailhead/parking/campsite area.

The Mill Creek Wilderness is 3m past the viewpoint. Also, back at the end of the pavement turn to see the Brennan Palisades (about .75m)

Wildlife Spectacle

52
- Only in Sept., Oct., and Nov.
- Various Lakes

Kokanee Spawn

In color on back cover.

Kokanee are land-locked salmon which spend their entire lives in lakes, unlike anadromous salmon which hatch in rivers, live as adults in the ocean, then return to their natal waters to spawn and die. Kokanee spawn and die either in their lake's tributaries or along a gravelly shoreline.

The spawn is interesting to see because all the fish turn bright red while males grow a gnarly fanged and hook-jawed mouth. Watch hundreds of these colored fish chasing and splashing as they battle for mating rights in the eddies and pools of a crystal-clear stream. One of nature's finest shows, and often only an arm's length from your very eyes! Central Oregon has some of the Northwest's premier kokanee lakes. In the summer the fish are relentlessly pursued by fishermen, but beginning in late Sept. the mating show is the ticket!

Shelter Cove Resort, Odell Lake.

Paulina Lake: (Entry 12) Usually mid-October. The lake has no tributaries so the stocked kokanee crowd the lakeshore near Paulina Lodge, or, in an odd phenomenon, hundreds end up downstream of the creek spillgate in a large pool. Where do the fish go after hatching? They can't swim upstream through the spillway and downstream is an 80-foot waterfall… weird…the fingerlings must plummet to their death …oops.

Paulina Creek bridge.

The Metolius River: Upstream from Billy Chinook Reservoir (entries 42&48). Usually in late September the fish migrate from the lake upstream to the headwaters. Take a peek from the Camp Sherman bridge, or better yet, from the river's edge adjacent to the "Riverside Tent-Camp" area (just downstream from The Head of the Metolius at the next dirt road). You can't see much from The Head.

Suttle Lake: In late September the fish migrate up Link Creek towards Blue Lake. Difficult to view because of private lands and brushy creek banks. Suttle Lake is 13m west of Sisters, and Link Creek is at the far end.

Odell Lake: This is the latest running spawn – from early October thru Thanksgiving. Truly an awe-inspiring Oregon spectacle as billions of bald eagles migrate here to feast on the lake's late-spawning bounty. See entry 14 for details!

WHATEVER WHATEVER WHATEVER WHATEVER WHATEVER WHATEVER WHATEVER WHATEVER WHATEVER

According to the Official Visitor's Guide to Bend, 2004, the dog population of Bend is 18,000.

DRIVE TOUR 1 – Cascade Lakes Highway

Bend's premier tour route! An 80-mile loop of quintessential High Cascades splendor – magnificent snow-capped peaks and lakes galore. A photo-op around every corner, a hike for every taste, and three lakeside resorts providing food, drinks, and boat rentals. Completing the loop you can visit Sunriver or any of the lavaland attractions along Hwy 97 back to Bend.

Map: The numbered circles correspond to *Bend Overall*'s entries. The lettered squares are other places of interest.

A: FS 41 to Deschutes River recreation sites.
B: FS 45, shortcut to Sunriver.

Elk Lake Lodge.

C: MP 32 – Elk Lake Resort. Food, restaurant, cabins, campground, gas, boat rentals.
D: MP 34 – Elk Lake beach – big and sandy.

Elk Lake.

E: MP 38 – Lava Lake Lodge. Groceries, campground, showers, boat rentals, gas.

Lava Lake Lodge.

F: MP 38 – Little Lava Lake. Headwaters of the Deschutes River to the right of the boatramp.

Lava Lake.

G: MP 44 – turn here onto FS 40 towards Sunriver.
H: MP 12 on FS 40 – Wake Butte Trail. Steep half-mile trail to odd rock formations (palagonite tuff resulting from magma rising up and encountering groundwater, causing an exlosion of cement-like goo that later solidified into peculiar angled striations).

(**Note:** you can extend this tour a bit by continuing past Crane Prairie Reservoir to MP 53 where you'll turn right to head back to Sunriver on FS 42).

Wake's palagonite.

I: MP 45 – Cultus Lake Resort. Groceries, gas, restaurant, cabins, campgrounds, boat rentals. Cultus is the only natural lake in the area that allows all watercraft – jetski, Hobie-cat, wakeboard boats, fishing – everything goes on this busy lake.

J: MP 47 – Quinn River Campground. Big campground. The Quinn River springs forth at campsite #30, next to the .75m trail to Osprey Point raptor viewing area.

K: MP 53 – turn left onto FS 42.

L: MP 16 on FS 42 – Fall River Springs. Park at the guard station. Springs gush forth on both sides of the building, creating an instant Fall River.

M: MP 15 – Fall River Campground. Riverside trail and bridge.

N: MP 10 – Fall River's falls. Turn right onto FS 4360 and drive .75m to parking on nearside of river. A trail leads 5 min downstream to falls (see entry 10).

O: Hwy 97 intersection. Turn left for twelve miles back to Bend.

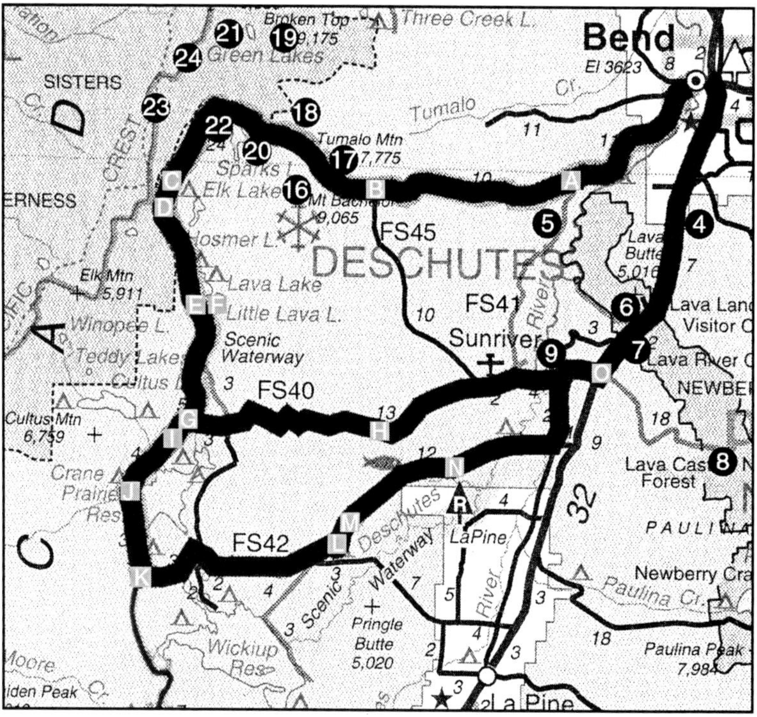

DRIVE TOUR 2 – McKenzie/Santiam Loop

One of the most beautiful drives in the country! Beginning and ending in Sisters, this 90 mile loop (3 hours minimum) features **everything** that makes Central Oregon unique. Spacious "dry-side" ponderosa forests, expansive black lava flows, long-ranging Cascade crest vistas, dense "wet-side" Douglas fir/cedar/maple forest, stunning waterfalls, crystal-clear lakes and rivers, lava tubes, plus historical landmarks with interpretive signs. Whew!

Drive the loop clockwise from Sisters to get the slower, trickier driving over McKenzie pass done while you are more fresh and patient. This way you end with a fast cruise into Sisters on Hwy 20 amongst the wonderful ponderosas – a welcome respite from the twists and turns of Hwys 242 and 126.

Highlights on this tour are marked with lettered squares. The numbered circles refer to entries in this guide.

A: Starting point at Hwy 242/ 20 split. This is MP 92 on Hwy 242.

B: MP 81. Windy Point viewpoint. According to the *Bend Bulletin* in Sept 1927…Shysters staged a fake goldrush at this andesite outcropping. An assayer set up shop and claims were bought into by the gullible. Bend's Paul Hosmer exposed the fraud in a few days when he sneaked in some worthless Bend basalt which was then assayed as "gold-bearing". (From Hatton's *Oregon's Sisters Country*).

C: MP 78. Dee Wright Observatory. Check entry 31.

D: MP 75. Craig memorial. Memorial gravesite and signage about a pioneer mailman.

E: MP 72. Scott Lake. Drive one mile to the end of the road and then take a short walk to see a premier view of the Three Sisters reflected in the lake.

F: MP 55. Junction with Hwy 126. For food head left for 5m, for gas 8m. There's no other gas on this route

G: MP 15 (on Hwy 126). Deer Creek Road. Little-known hot spring on McKenzie's bank.

Scott Lake.

H: MP 12. Trail Bridge Reservoir. *The Bend Bulletin*, 1955, opined "Nature and beauty lovers are bucking this project, but up to now they haven't been strongly enough organized to make themselves heard effectively. Its to be hoped they do get organized, and force the city of Eugene to prove absolute necessity before grinding up that priceless scenery into a few hundred kilowatts."

Notice spring-fed waterfalls along the Hwy, just past the entrance.

I: MP 0. Junction with Hwy 20 – go right.

J: Junction with Hwy 22 – stay right. Begin climb and as you approach Hogg Rock, near MP 78, look up on the rocky hillside. This is the site of a late-1800s ill-fated railroad venture. Portions of the railgrade are still visible.

K: MP 80. Hoodoo Ski Area, Big Lake, and the Pacific Crest Trail.

L: MP 81. In 2003, the B and B complex forest fire, largest in Deschutes Nat'l Forest history, began near here at Booth Lake.

M: MP 84. Mt. Washington viewpoint and interpretive signs.

N: MP 87. Suttle Lake Resort and campgrounds. Food and drinks.

O: MP 92. Black Butte Ranch.
MP 100. Back into Sisters.

Mt. Washington Viewpoint.

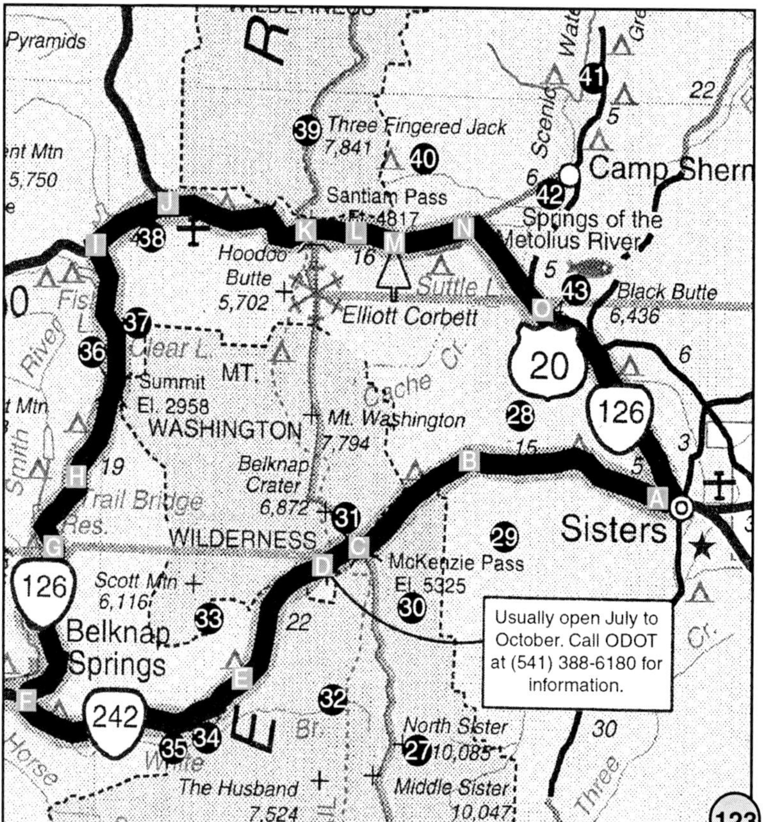

DRIVE TOUR 3 – Rocks and Irrigation

This 90-120 mile tour takes you on a loop north towards Madras. Allow 4-6 hours, depending on curiosity.

GEOLOGIC HIGHLIGHTS: Smith Rock State Park's stunning geography – towering colorful rock walls, the flowing Crooked River, and wildlife viewing. An option to visit Richardson's Roc ranch to dig for the state's best thundereggs. Over to Lake Billy Chinook to visit the sparkling blue waters impounded by sheer basalt walls. A stop at the P.S. Ogden wayside to walk the old Crooked River Bridge over its 300-foot gorge. And, to finish, check out Petersen Rock Gardens' collection of crafted rock oddities.

IRRIGATION: Central Oregon would not be the same without the massive irrigation fueled by the Deschutes' amazingly consistent flow rate. Local irrigation is older than the town of Bend, yet its story is seldom told or understood.

Since this geologic tour passes by, near, over, and around the systems of irrigation – dams, canals, tunnels, reservoirs, and sprinklers – here's an overview of the interesting journey the Deschutes' water takes between Crane Prairie and Wickiup reservoirs and the watered fields of Redmond and Madras.

The tour starts at the North Unit diversion dam in Bend (built by private interests in 1912) where three canals simultaneously draw their water from the river. The first is the North Main Unit that can convey up to 1000 cfs to Madras. The second is the Pilot Butte canal (up to 500 cfs) that zigs and zags near and under Hwy 97 as it waters most of Redmond. The third, smaller canal is the 100+ year-old Swalley flume that carries about 100 cfs of water northwest of Bend.

Note the amount of water left in the river after the canals: generally the summer flow at Benham Falls is about 1500 cfs before the irrigators withdraw their allotment. The canal operators (upstream also) divert all but about 50 cfs, which they let pass over the diversion dam. They have a gentlemen's agreement to let that much pass in order to keep the Deschutes flowing. Mid-century the river was sometimes left completely dry.

The most interesting story is the North Main Unit canal. The Bureau of Reclamation built Wickiup Res. between 1939 and 1949 to store the Unit's water. The stored water flows as the Deschutes River before entering the canal, where it begins a 65-mile journey to Madras. Only gravity is needed to get it from Bend's 3623 elev. to the 2400 elev. of the Madras plains. On its way it crosses *over* the Crooked River gorge via a 520-foot concrete bridge and flume (built in 1944-46 when steel was scarce during WW2). Then the canal meets Smith Rock where two tunnels (totaling 1.3 miles) were blasted under the rocks to carry the water. Emerging from the tunnels, the canal goes under Hwy 97, around Juniper Butte, and back under the Hwy again on its way into Haystack Res. Haystack serves to regulate the flow, via 235 miles of lateral canals, into the sprinklers of Madras, Culver, and Metolius.

Strange but true! Virtually every sprinkler you see on this whole tour is squirting water taken at the diversion dam in Bend!

A: Riverview Park (Drive Tour 4, #4), overlooks swan pond and the dam canals. On Division, north of Revere before Bus. 97. To get on Hwy 97 north, go left on Bus. 97 then right on Empire to quickly loop onto the Hwy.

B: Veterans Way (.5m S of Redmond one-way). Notice Pilot Butte canal on west side of Hwy and crossing under just before one-way split. ALSO, on the return trip, you'll turn here to head to Petersen's.

C: Terrebonne. At the flashing yellow light turn R onto B st. In .7m go left onto 1st for 2m to Smith entrance. (At Smith, to see the canal enter the tunnel, hike down to river, upstream 1m, then up the slope.)

D: North Main canal. Exiting Smith go left. In .9m you'll cross the canal. To the left, but not accessible, is the bridge over the Crooked that transports the water. Continuing, make the next left then soon left again onto Lone Pine road.

E: Cross the Crooked River.

F: Skull Hollow BLM campground/ Grey Butte trailhead. Go left when you get to Hwy 26.

G: Intersect Hwy 97 just south of Madras. For side-trip to Richardson's go right and consult entry 49. To continue, go left.

H: Iris Lane. Turn right, into Culver, then follow signs for Cove Palisades State Park. For rim viewpoints turn R before descending to lake. Once down at lake's marina, go L about 5m to see the Crooked arm, the Palisades, the Deschutes arm, and the "Deschutes Formation" strata. Retrace drive back to Hwy 97.

I: Jericho Lane (1m south of Iris). Go left 1.5m to visit Haystack – fishing pier canal works are neat.

J: MP 105.5. Cross over N. Main Unit canal. It comes from your right, after skirting Juniper Butte.
MP 109. Cross over canal again. Upstream are Smith's tunnels. Look for canal grade on hillside.

K: Crooked River Bridge/ Peter Skene Ogden viewpoint. Stop, read signs, walk over old Hwy bridge. Good photo-op south of the rail bridge.

B: Veterans Way. Turn R then immediately L onto SW Canal Blvd to visit Petersens and have a peek down into the Deschutes canyon. On SW Canal go 4m then R on McVey (at Petersen signs). In 1.4m slow and stop at a dirt pulloff to look down into the Deschutes canyon – note the meager flow, post canal-take. Continue 1m to Petersen's. From Gardens, go L, then L on Young to 2nd stopsign, then R to Hwy 97.

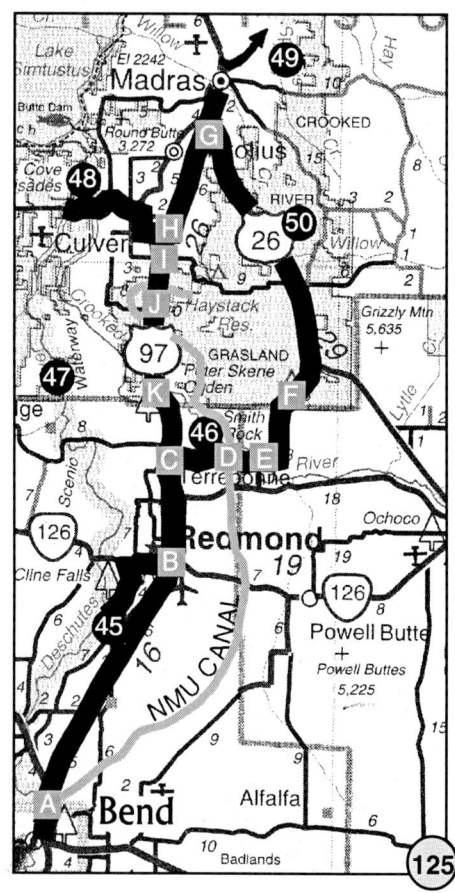

DRIVE TOUR 4 – Downtown Bend

1) **The Funny Farm:** Age-old landmark of quirkiness. Odd art sculptures, bizarre displays, odds 'n' ends for sale?! Free. Deschutes Market Road and Hwy 97.
2) **Tumalo State Park:** Family-picnic feel along the banks of the low-flow Deschutes (see tour 3). Tubers love to walk .5m upstream and float down. $3 state park fee. Take OB Riley Road west from Bend River Mall 4m.

   Tumalo State Park.
3) **Bend Visitor and Conv. Bureau:** All the maps and brochures you'll ever need. Good supply of *Bend Overall*, other guides, and momentos.
4) **Riverview Park:** Near to the North Unit diversion dam and its artificial waterfall (may soon be fenced). Read Tour 3 for details.

   North Unit diversion dam.
5) **Central Oregon Community College:** The "COCC on the rock", dedicated in 1965, is a beautiful hillside campus sporting outstanding Cascades views. And some Art.
6) **Shevlin Park:** Head west on Newport Ave. Huge forested park along Tumalo Creek. Running, biking, picnicking, finding your own remote solitude so close to town.
7) **Tumalo Falls:** Galveston Ave. leads to the falls – check entry 15.
8) **Bend Power and Light Dam:** Built in 1909 to create Bend's first electricity. It backs up the Deschutes into our famed and loved Mirror Pond. See dam from Newport Ave., see powerhouse behind Elks lodge.
9) **Pilot Butte:** Bend's 480-foot landmark – entry 1 for details.
10) **Juniper Park:** Vast city park. Playgrounds, swimming pool, tennis courts, baseball diamond, street hockey, horseshoes, walking trails, art, and more.
11) **Drake Park/Mirror Pond:** Grassy park with sidewalk trails meandering along the glassy Deschutes.
12) **Library:** On Wall St., one block south of Franklin Ave.
13) **DesChutes County Historical Center:** Great displays and photos detail local history. Peruse 100 years of *Bulletin* back issues. A terrific rainy-day outing – get to know the Bend that Was. $2.50
14) **McKay Park:** Grassy park along a swift-flowing section of Deschutes. Popular with dogs, waders, inner-tubers, frisbees, and sun-bathers.

    McKay Park.

15) **Art Station:** The original 1911 Bend railroad depot. Moved here because of Bend parkway. It's now an art workshop. Pop in the front door to read about the 1911 Bend time-capsule found during the move.
16) **Les Schwab Amphitheater:** Outdoor riverside concert venue. Part of Old Mill redevelopment. Brings the big music acts to little ol' Bend.
17) **Old Mill Redevelopment Riverside Parks:** Not quite finished as of 5/04, but they look to have nice meandering riverside trails.
18) **Mt Bachelor Village Riverside Trail:** .75m dirt trail leading upriver from Bill Healy bridge. Lots of gurgling rapids and a scad of informative signs along the untamed Deschutes.

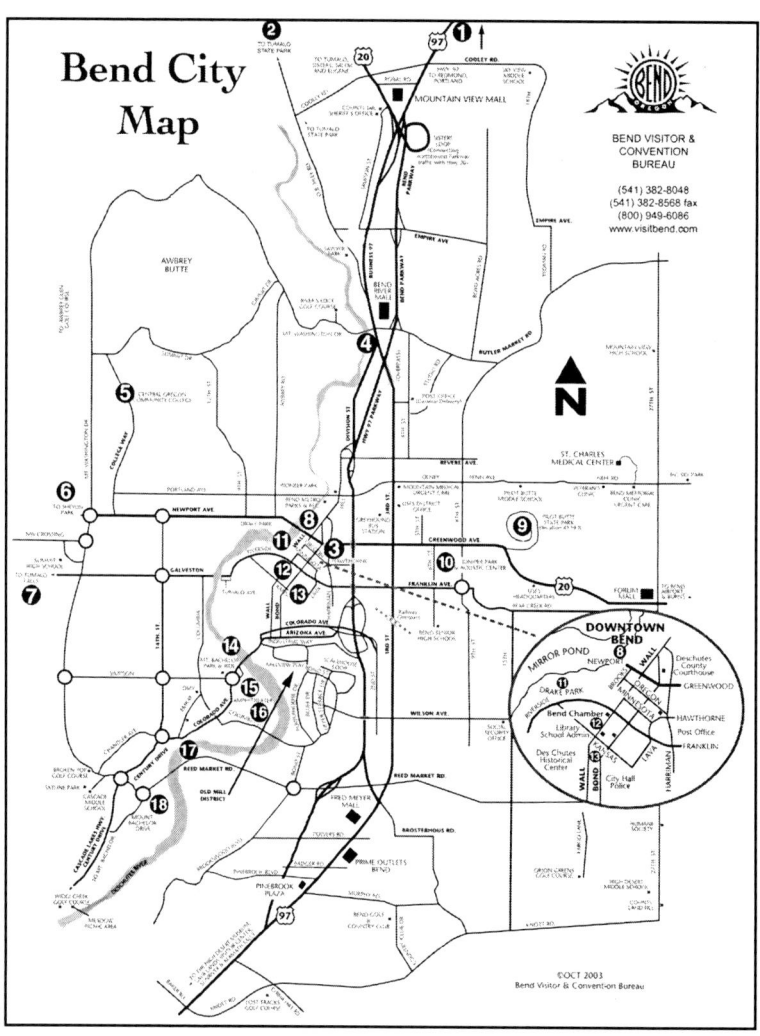

ART HUNT
Like 'em or hate 'em, you gotta find 'em!

_____

_____

_____

_____

_____

_____

_____

_____

_____

In most boomtowns the locals only have the crass new development to critique. But here in Bend we have lots of public art to criticize as well. Sweet!

Perhaps it takes the pressure off the developers – if they plunk some horrid obelisk in the roundabout in front of their cookie-cutter knock-ups, maybe we won't notice the golfsprawl. Just kidding…

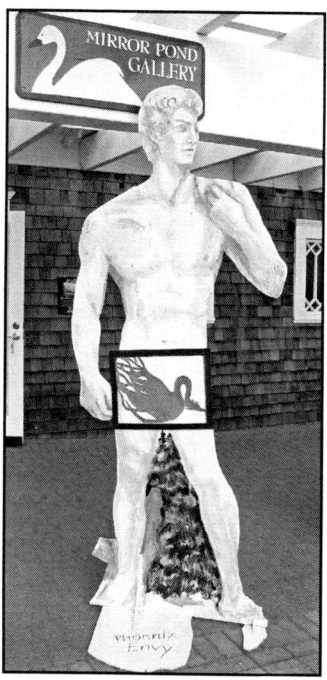

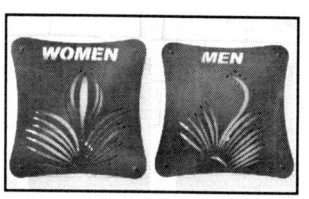

Conifer Identification in Central Oregon

Identifying the conifers around Bend overall is fairly easy, but it's still a fun challenge and an impressive feat to know them all. There are only about a dozen major tree types, and unlike some other regions, each of our trees has recognizable characteristics for the everyman – no need for super-close scrutiny to tell this region's trees apart. Once you learn a few clues to help with the comparing and contrasting, the ID is a snap! The fun challenge around here is when the harsh growing conditions – lava flows, cinder hills, pumice fields – interact with variable rainfall and altitude to torment the trees into surprising forms.

This guide is meant to be a down 'n' dirty crash course in conifers. If my clues don't do the job, I recommend two excellent easy-to-use books: *Trees to Know in Oregon* by Ross and Jensen for O.S.U., and Falcon's *Western Trees* by Stuckey and Palmer.

To start off, here's a list of our native conifers broken down into three groups:

LONG-NEEDLED BUNCHES	SINGLE-NEEDLES ALONG TWIG	SCALE LEAVES
Ponderosa pine	Douglas-fir	Juniper
Lodgepole pine	Englemann spruce	Incense cedar
Western white pine	Mtn hemlock	Western redcedar
Whitebark pine	True fir	
	Larch (Tamarack)	

Now here's a cross-section diagram generalizing where the trees grow according to east/west orientation, rainfall, and altitude:

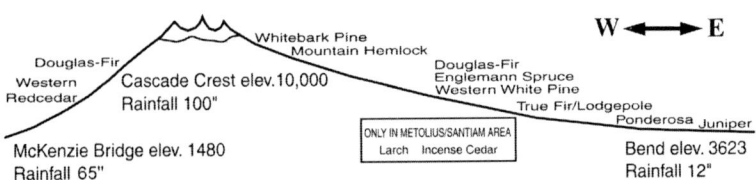

STARTING THE IDENTIFICATION PROCESS: Begin with the pines because they are the easiest. The four pines all have longish needles bunched towards the end of the branch (like a brush), whereas the single-needle trees sport shorter needles all along the twig (like teddybear arms).

True fir, WW pine.

Pine, single-needle.

Pine Characteristics:

Ponderosa: Long needles in bunches of three. Large woody cones. Mature bark is orange, young bark is blackish. Elev. range 3,000-6,500 ft.

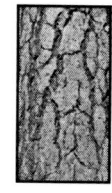

Lodgepole: Short needles in bunches of two. Small, 2-3 inch cones have a flattened side. Bark is gray, thin, and scaly. Elev. Range 3,000-8,000 ft.

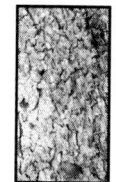

Western white: Needles in bunches of five. Cones are 6-8 inches and shaped like bananas. Mature bark forms a squared "alligator-skin" pattern, young bark is gray and scaly. Elev. Range 4,000-7,000 ft.

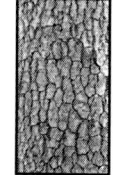

Whitebark: Needles in bunches of five. Cones are egg-sized. Only grows at alpine treeline (6,000-8,000 ft) and is often short and contorted due to wind and snow.

Scale-leaf tree Characteristics:

Juniper: Desert tree - grows everywhere east of Bend. Sometimes contorted and short, other times tall and straight. Little blue berries. Foliage is somewhat bushy, whereas the cedars' foliage splays flatly.

Incense cedar: The "dry-side" cedar. Twigs splay flatly and angle sharply forward. Small duck-bill shaped cone. Not as droopy looking as the redcedar, nor is the vertical bark as stringy. Mostly grows in the Metolius river vicinity.

Western redcedar: The "wet-side" cedar. Droopy foliage. Small and plentiful rosebud-shaped cones. Very stringy vertical bark that can be peeled into long strips. Mostly grows at lower elevations on the west side of the passes.

Single-Needled Characteristics:

Now comes the hard part – *the single-needled trees are the trickiest ones. Learning these five will definitely separate the casual outdoorsman from the tree guru!*

- Douglas-fir
- Englemann spruce
- Mountain hemlock
- True fir
- Larch

First, a word about true firs. There are actually five firs in the area: white, silver, grand, noble, and subalpine. They give IDers fits because they interbreed and mix attributes, becoming unidentifiable. Thus, experts often just lump them all as "true firs". Stuckey and Palmer say, "It is fairly easy to know that a tree in question is a fir; if the question is, which fir, it isn't so easy." Ross and Jensen comment, "…several of our species interbreed, resulting in offspring that have characteristics of both parents."

If you want to really try to ID the true firs, you better get a real tree book and prepare for confusion.

By the way, Douglas-fir is not a true fir. It is a psuedo-hemlock with down-hanging cones and spiraled needles, but a stiff tip.

That said, these five trees all have branches covered with single needles. (The larch is a bit unique so I'll talk about it at the end). The first features to look for on these trees are the cones – this is how you distinguish a true fir from a mtn hemlock/Englemann spruce/Douglas-fir. A true fir only has cones on its very top branches in the late summer/fall. Also, fir cones sit upright on the branches, whereas on the other trees the cones all hang downwards. And, most importantly, the cones of a true fir do not fall to the ground intact – they disintegrate into flakes while still on the branch. So, on the ground under a true fir you won't find a bunch of cones (like under a Doug/Engle/Hem), but just some triangular flakes. The bark on true firs varies from ridged gray/black to smoothish gray with blisters.

Upright cone & flakes.

Under a Doug/Engle/Hem you'll find millions of cones and you'll also see plentiful down-hanging cones throughout the trees, year-round. So, if there are cones on the ground, it's not a true fir, and the trick to IDing a Douglas-fir from a Mountain hemlock or Englemann spruce is to examine a cone, then verify the ID with a look at the bark, tip, or needles.

Mountain hemlock –
Cone: 2-3 inches, darkish color, scales are rounded and often bent down.
Bark: Dark gray, thick, deep vertical ridges and furrows. Needles are short – .75 inches.

Englemann spruce –
Cone: 2-3 inches, yellow-orange color, thin papery scales.
Bark: Thin, gray, and very flaky/ scaly. Needles are 1-1.5 inches and sharp.

Douglas-fir –
Cone: 2-4 inches, unique and distinctive 3-pronged pitchfork-like "bracts".
Bark: Dark gray or brown, thick, deep vertical ridges and furrows. Needles are long,1.5 inches, and softish.

Hemlock
Englemann
Douglas

MORE TRICKS: The tips of hemlocks all droop over. This is unique – Doug/Eng/True/Larch tips all point straight up.

An Englemann's needles are sharp – grab a twig and you'll say "ouch!" The other trees have no-ouch needles.

Drooping hemlocks.

Now the **larch**, often called a tamarack. The larch is the only deciduous conifer – its needles turn bright yellow in autumn, fall off in the winter, and regrow a bright green color in the spring. One of the best places to get to know a larch is the Jack Creek area. The larch grows arrow-straight and tall, has dark, furrowed bark like a young ponderosa, and unique needles that grow in clusters off "pegs" along the twig.

GOOD PLACES TO EXAMINE TREES:

Tumalo Falls: Across the river from the top viewpoint, four trees gather at the falls – ponderosa, lodgepole, true fir, and an Englemann. Now look left to see a droopy-tipped hemlock.
Jack Creek area: Ponderosa, Douglas-fir, larch, Englemann spruce, incense cedar, true fir, and more! Head up to Jack Lake to see lodgepole, mtn hemlock, and a W. white pine (along the lakeshore).
Cultus Lake resort: Lots and lots.

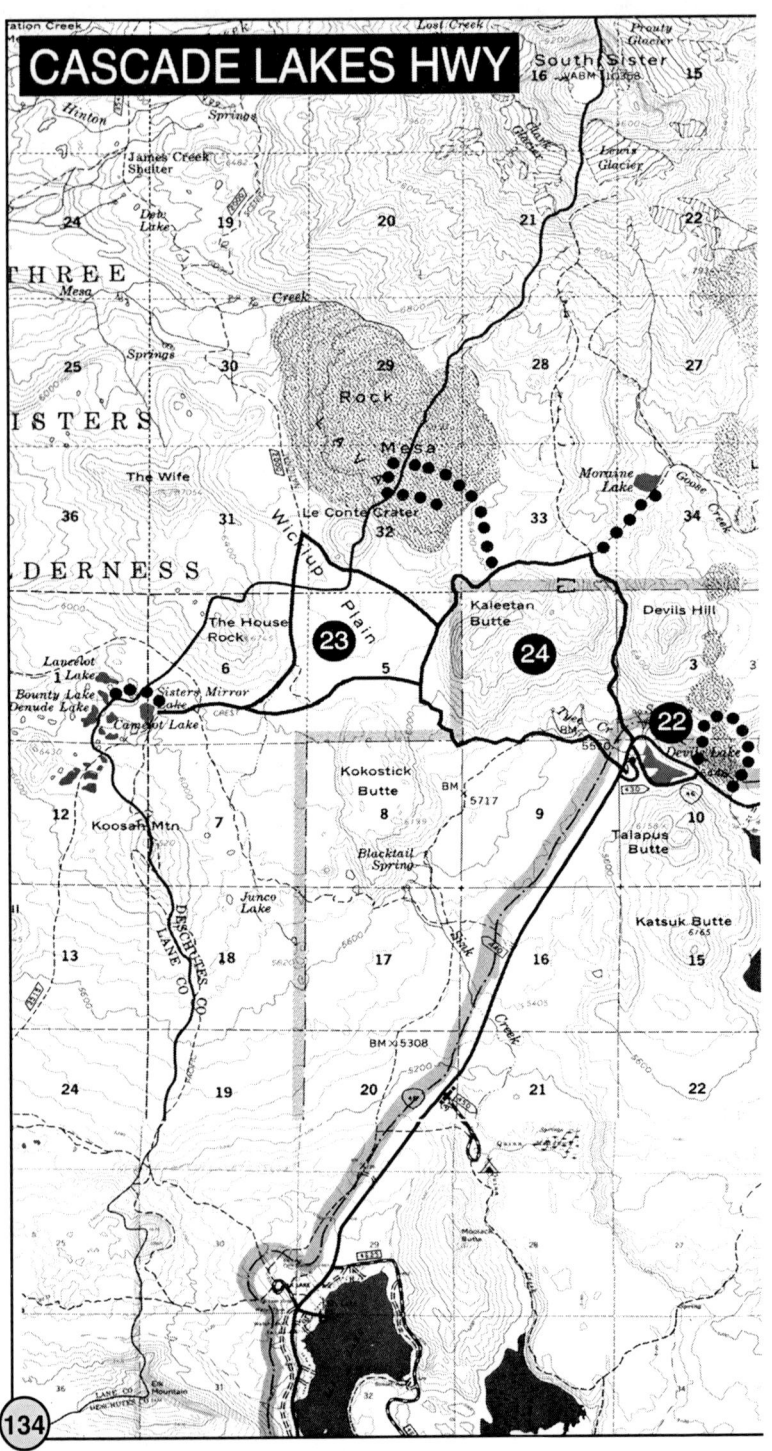

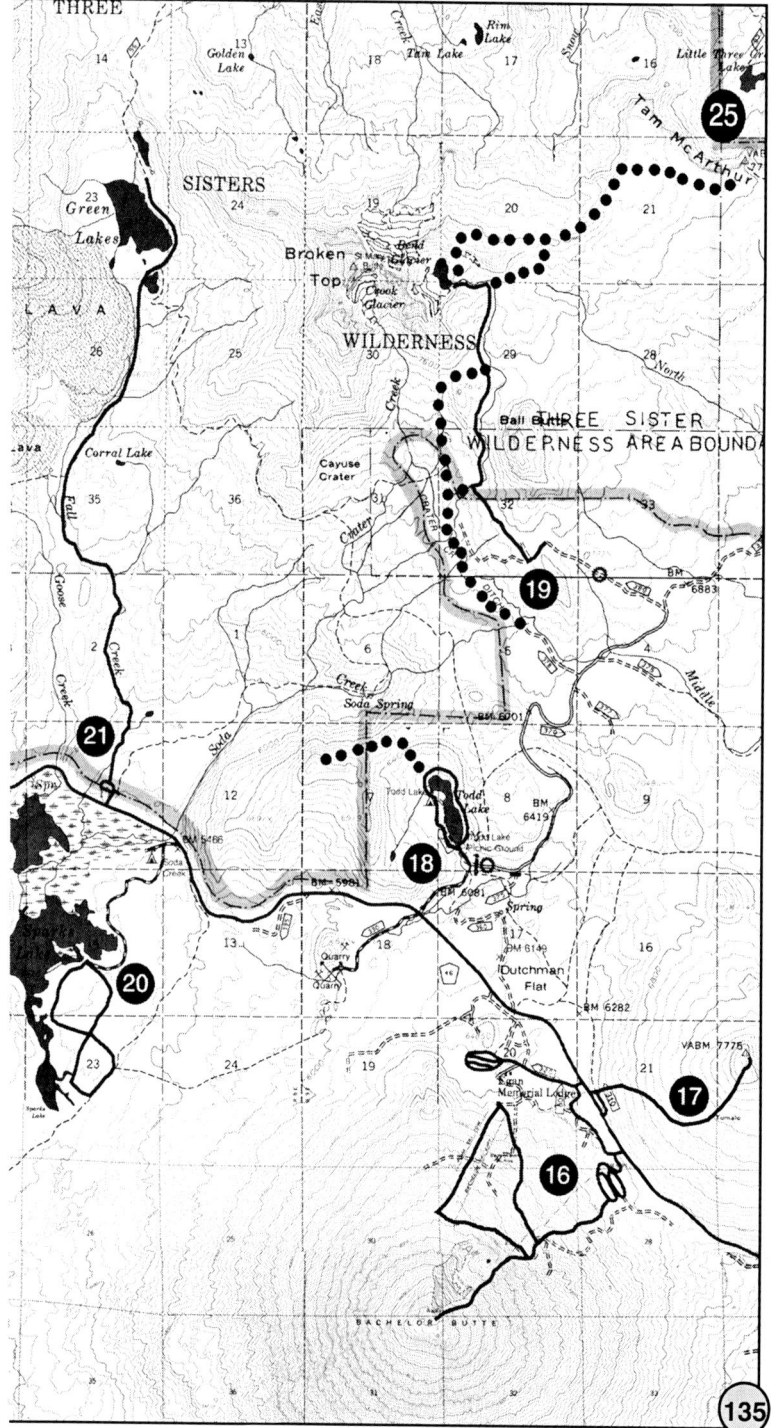

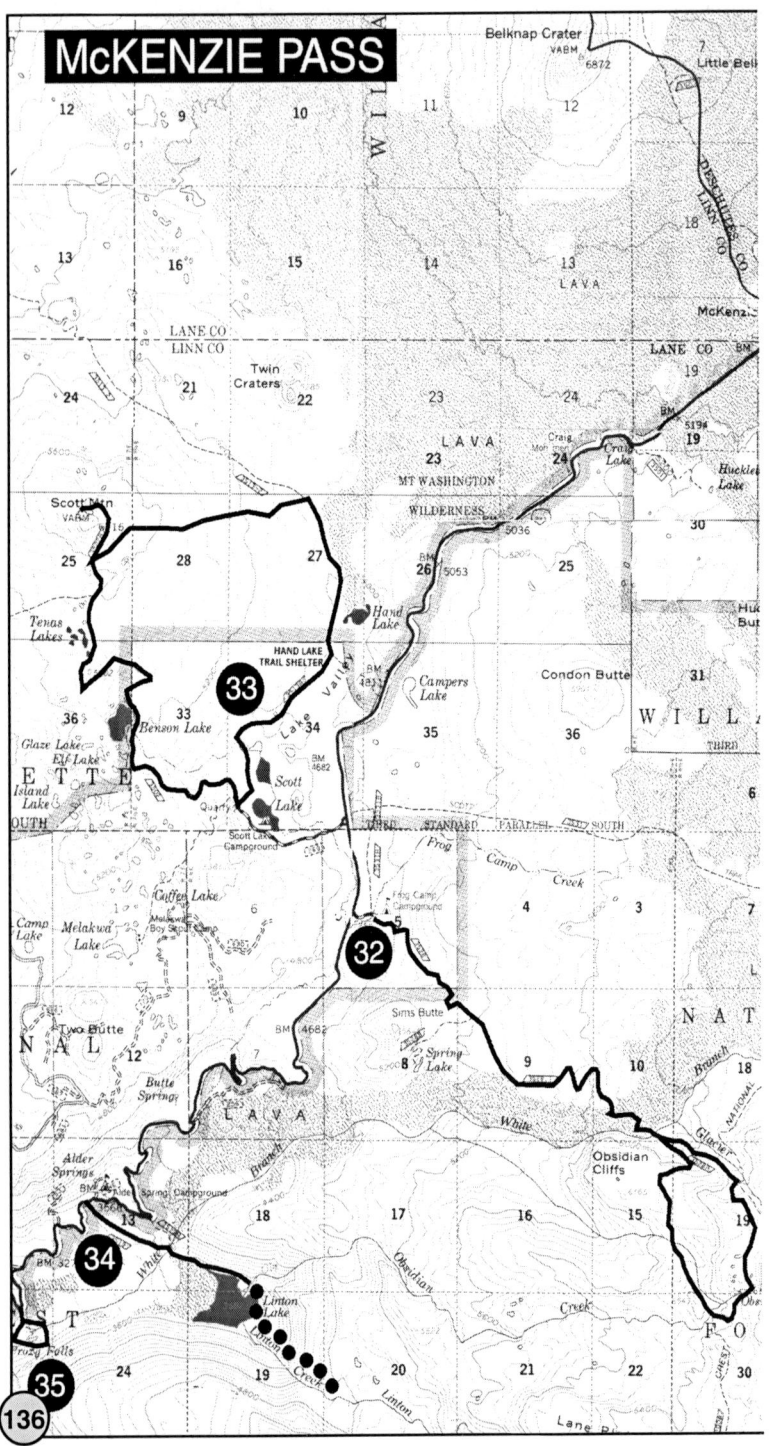

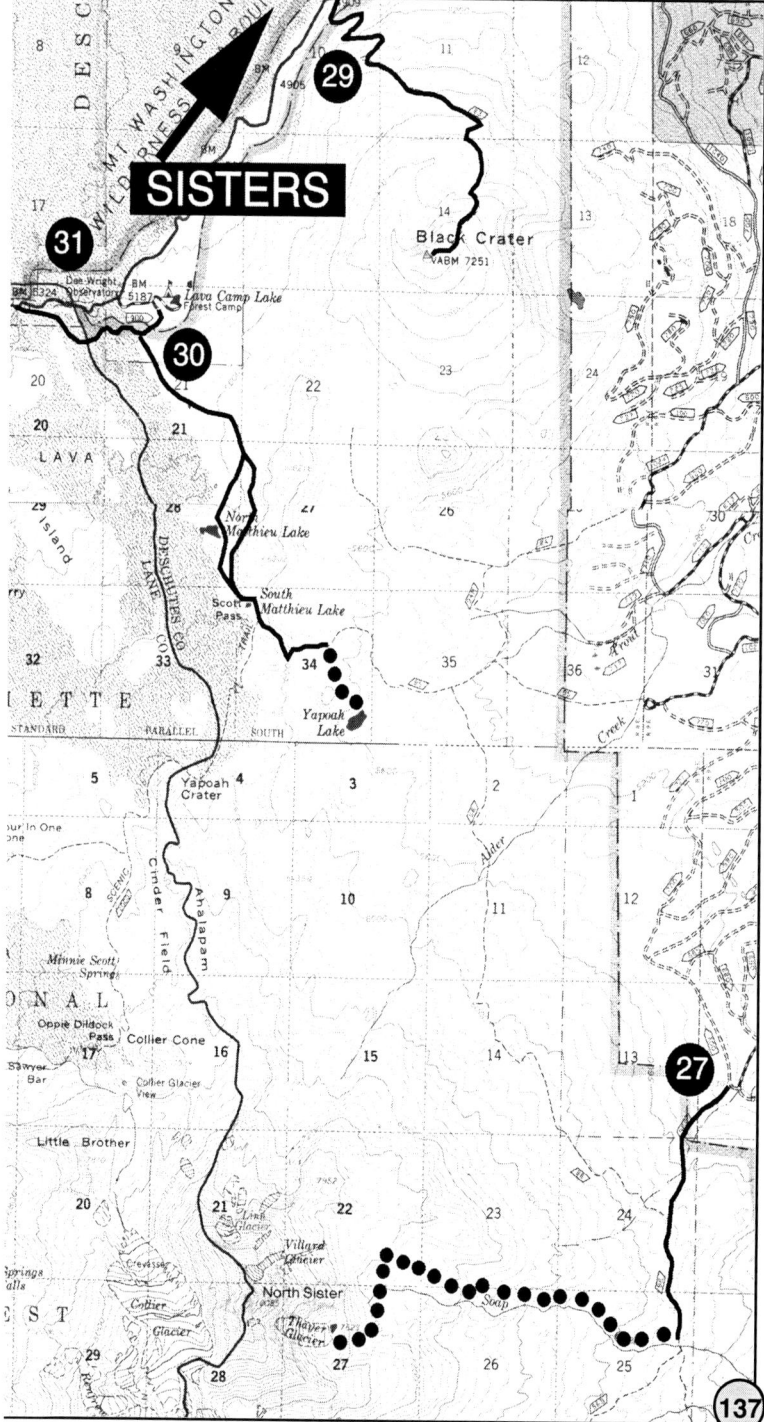

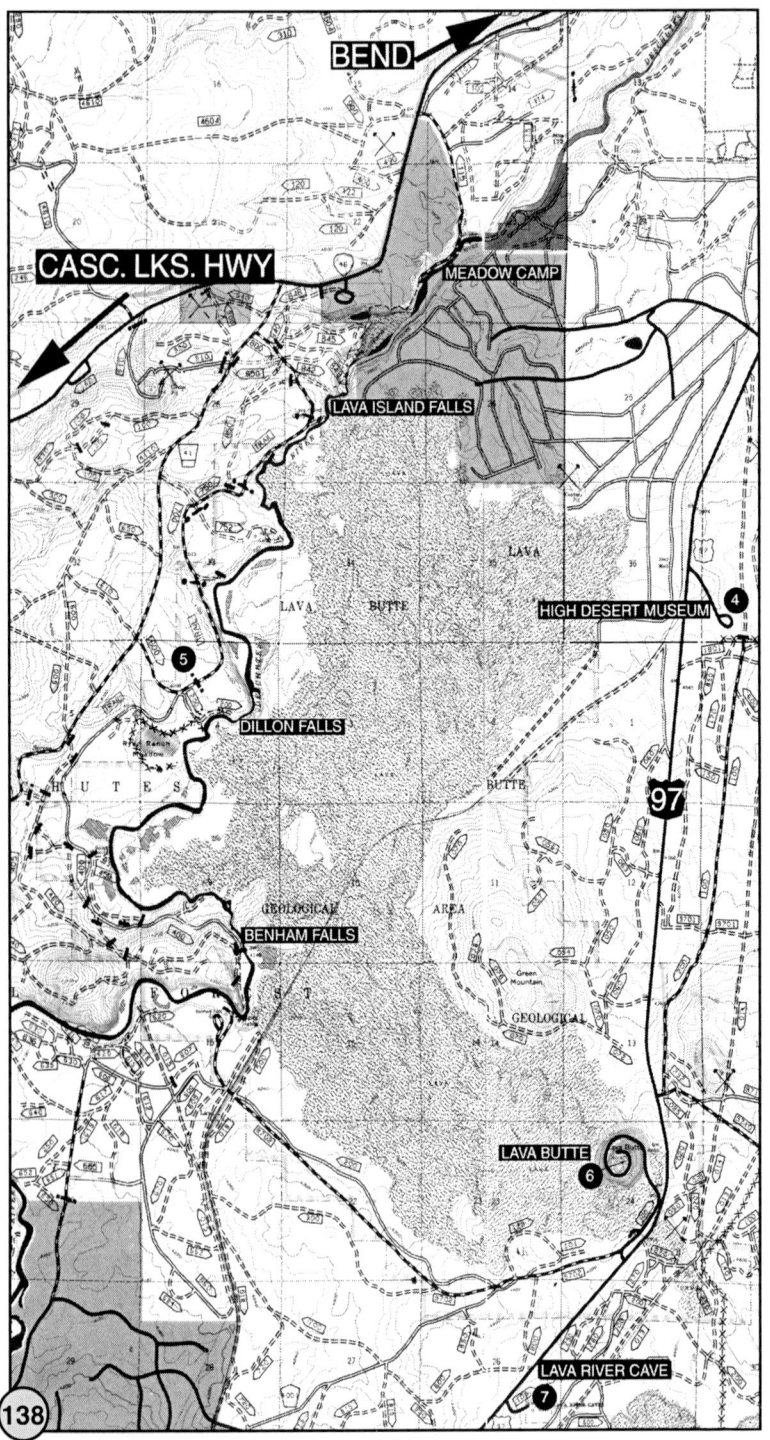

CANYON CREEK MEADOWS

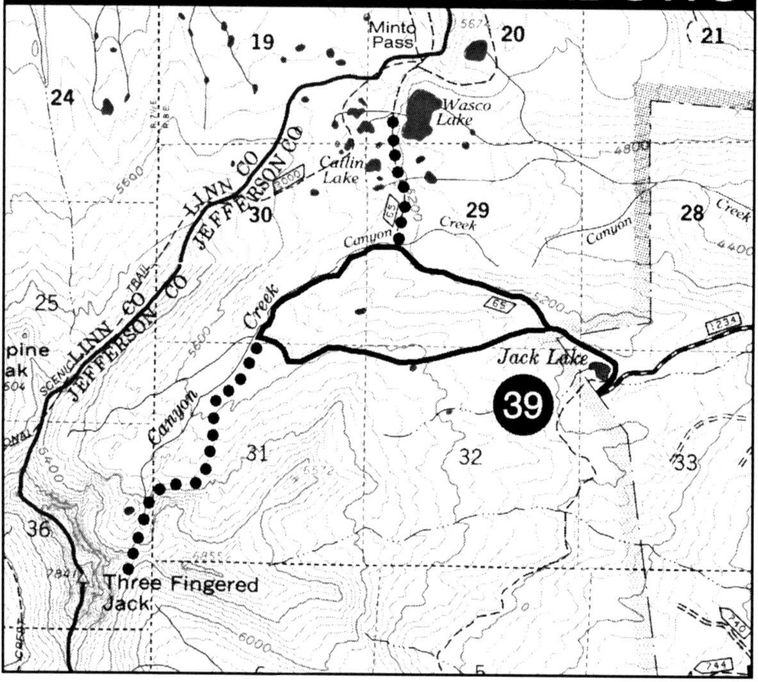

MAP OF NEWBERRY CALDERA AREA

Available at the entrance station.

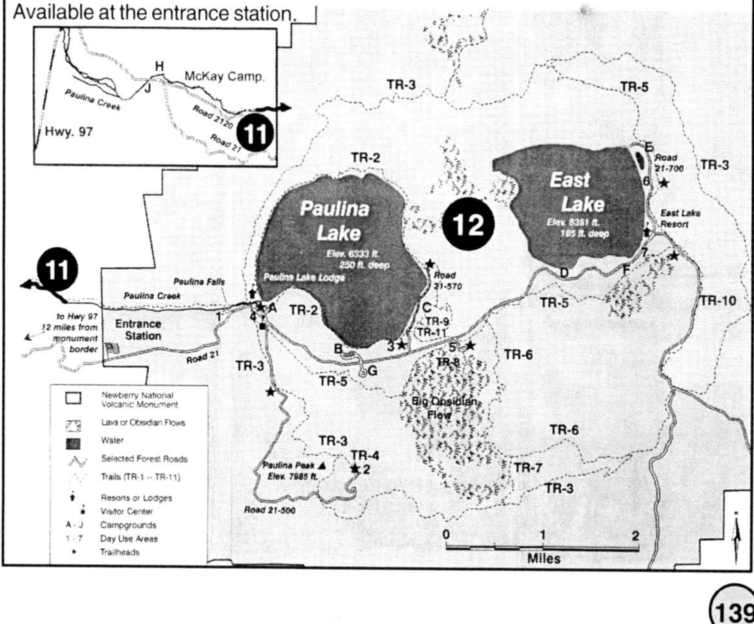

SQUAW CREEK/TAM McARTHUR RIM

NOTES

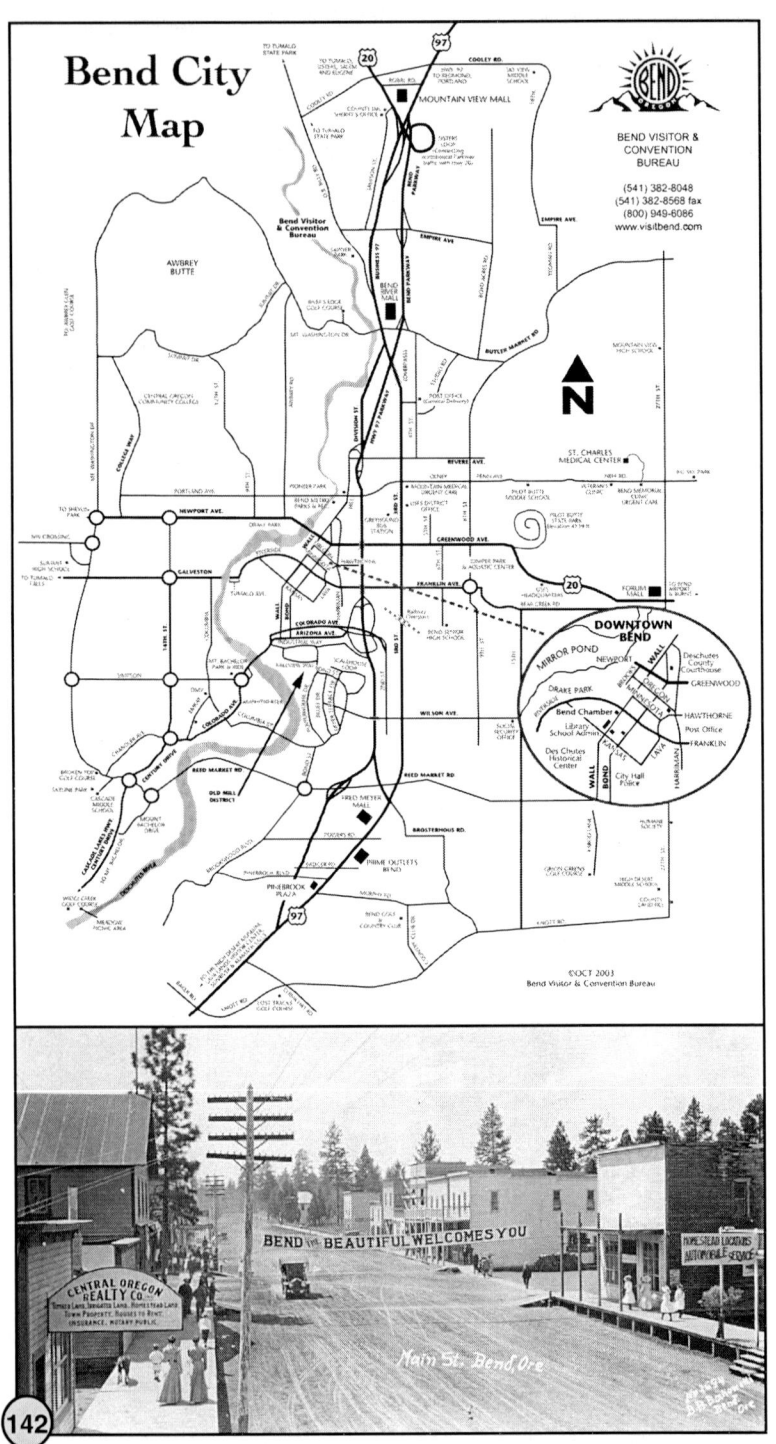

Time Estimate MATRIX

Round-Trip Time Estimate from Bend (includes drive)

Time	Destination	Scenic Hike	Mtn Views	Waterfalls	Lakes	Unique Attraction	Drive Time (one-way)	Dogs	Fee
.5 Hr	Mirror Pond				●	●	3	Y	
	McKay Park					●	4	Y	
	Pilot Butte - drive (1)		●				6	L	
	Town Tour								
1.0 Hr	Tumalo Falls View (15)			●			15	L	
	Pilot Butte Hike (1)						6	L	
	Deschutes River Sites (5)	●					10	L	●
	Boyd Cave - sample (3)					●	12	N	
	Lava Butte (6)	●	●			●	9	L	●
	Petersen Rock Gardens (45)					●	11	L	
	LaPine S.P.-Big Tree view (10)					●	26	Y	
1.5 Hrs	Boyd or Skeleton Cave (3)					●	12	N	
	Head of the Metolius (42)		●			●	35	L	
	Todd Lake (18)	●	●		●		25	L	●
	Sparks Lake (20)	●	●		●		27	Y	
	Lava Cast Forest (8)	●	●			●	30	L	
2 Hrs	Sunriver Nature Center (9)					●	18	N	
	Lava River Cave (7)					●	10	N	●
	Dee Wright Observatory (31)	●	●			●	40	L	
	Wizard Falls Hatchery (41)					●	45	L	
	Skylight Cave (28)					●	40	N	
	Sawyers Cave (38)					●	51	N	
	Head of the Jack (40)	●					40	Y	
	Dry River Gorge (2)	●					20	Y	
2.5 Hrs	Rimrock Springs (50)	●	●				46	L	
	Devils Lake (22)	●			●		30	Y	●
	Tumalo Mtn (17)	●	●				23	Y	
	Mt. Bachelor - Chairlift (16)		●			●	24	N	●
	Sahalie/Koosah Falls (36)	●		●			60	Y	
	Proxy Falls (35)	●		●			60	Y	
3 Hrs	Smith Rock S.P. (46)	●	●				28	L	●
	Steelhead Falls (47)	●		●			43	Y	
	High Desert Museum (4)					●	5	N	●
	LaPine S.P. Hike/Bike (10)	●	●				26	Y	
	Tumalo Falls - Hike (15)	●		●			15	Y	●
	Metolius River Canyon (41)	●					45	Y	
3.5 Hrs	Mt. Bachelor-Summit Hike (16)	●	●				23	Y	
	Alder Springs (44)	●					41	Y	
	Squaw Creek Falls (26)	●		●			60	Y	
	Sisters Mirror Lakes (23)	●	●		●		30	Y	●
	Rock Mesa/Moraine Lake (24)	●	●		●		30	L	●
	Matthieu Lakes (30)	●	●		●		40	Y	
	Richardsons Rec. Ranch (49)					●	60	Y/N	
	Clear Lake (37)	●	●		●		57	Y	
	Steins Pillar (51)	●					60	Y	
	Paulina Creek Falls (11)	●		●			28	Y	
	Fort Rock/Hole ITG (13)	●					70	Y	
	Tam McArthur Rim (25)	●	●		●		50	Y	●
4.0 Hrs	Black Butte (43)	●	●				44	Y	●
	Linton Lake & Falls (34)	●		●	●		59	Y	
	Newberry Caldera (12)	●	●	●	●	●	36	Y	
	Broken Top (19)	●	●		●		45	L	
	Green Lakes (21)	●	●		●		28	Y	
	Black Crater (29)	●	●				36	Y	
5 Hrs	Canyon Creek Meadows (39)	●	●	●			60	Y	●
	Lake Billy Chinook (48)	●	●		●	●	42	L	●
	Tenas Lakes/Scott Mtn (33)	●	●		●		50	Y	●
6 Hrs	Obsidian Trail (32)	●	●			●	51	Y	●
	North Sister - Thayer Lake (27)	●	●		●		43	Y	●
	Odell Lake Wildlife (14)				●	●	90	Y	

Visiting Bend?

Here is a list of Bend's top attractions, in no order. These outings will be the ones that impress the friends back home. BUY THIS GUIDE. Hurry and get going! Don't waste time trying to wade through all the free brochures - their directions often suck. *Bend, Overall* will get you there and give you the info you need to experience the true uniqueness of Bend.

WEEKEND VISIT

PILOT BUTTE: (entry #1) (20 min – 1 hr) For a premier 360° view of Bend and the Cascades either drive to the top (summer), or hike the trail.

LAVA RIVER CAVE: (entry #7) (2 hrs) The daddy of Central Oregon's lava tubes. Lantern rentals and full-time rangers on site.

DESCHUTES RIVER sites: (entry #5) (45 min – 2 hrs) The River that defines Bend. See its raging, undamned, and unspoiled beauty.

TUMALO FALLS: (entry #15) (1-3 hrs) Bend's landmark waterfall, the cover of this guide.

LAVA BUTTE: (entry #6) (1-2 hrs) The "volcano" cinder-cone that rises from south Hwy 97. Both a fascinating natural attraction and the site of Newberry Mnmt's visitor center. Don't miss it!

DRIVE the CASCADE LAKES HWY past MT BACHELOR: (Drive tour 1, pg 120) (1.5-3 hrs) A 25m journey to the photogenic heart of the Cascades. Definitely plan to stop at Todd (18), Sparks (20), or Devils Lake (22). Don't leave Bend without doing this!

IN SISTERS?? Visit Head of the Metolius (entry #42) or Three Creeks Lake (entry #25).

WEEK LONG VISIT

SMITH ROCK STATE PARK: (entry #46) (half day) Unbelievable scenery. Hiking galore, world-class rock-climbing, wildlife viewing. GO!

NEWBERRY CALDERA NAT'L MNMT: (entry #12) (all day) National Park gah-gah without the crowds. Something for everyone – hike, drive, boat, fish, eat.

THE HIGH DESERT MUSEUM: (entry #4) (3 hrs) A wildlife extravaganza with culture and history to boot.

PETERSEN ROCK GARDENS: (entry #45) (1.5 hrs) A quirky place for a budget family outing or for curiosity seekers.

DRIVE the McKENZIE/ SANTIAM HWYS loop: (drive tour 2, pg 122) (4-6 hrs) Must-see Oregon splendor. Unsurpassed beauty and interest. WOW! Unforgettable!

PLAY IN THE DESCHUTES RIVER

WHITEWATER RAFT TRIPS: A Bend classic - 2 hours of fun for about $40. Only two companies: Sun Country Tours (541-382-6277) or Inn of the 7th Mtn (541-382-8711).

INNER-TUBE from the OLD MILL to MIRROR POND: Bend's newest hot summer fun! Drift from Bill Healy bridge to McKay Park then on to Mirror Pond. Alder Creek Kayaks will rent and sell tubes in '05.

Details at downtown Vis. Ctr. or Alder Creek Kayaks (downstairs in the Mill A bldg where Colorado Ave crosses the river 541-317-9407)